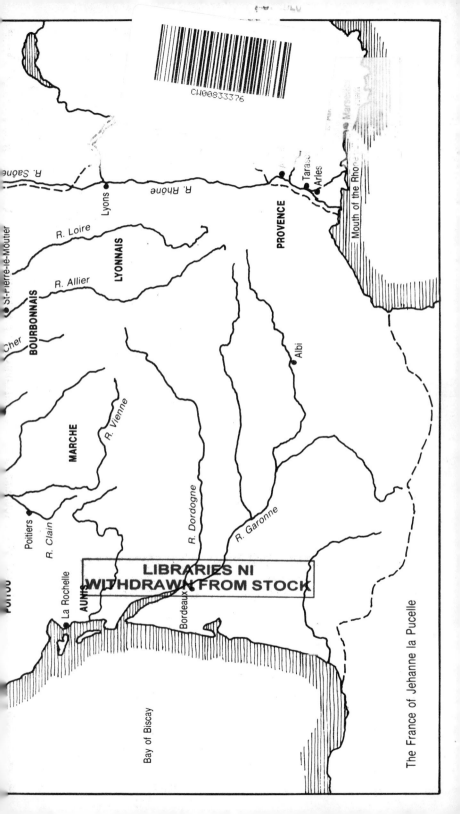

The France of Jehanne la Pucelle

The Real Joan of Arc?

The fireplace discovered in the salon of Jaulny Castle with the portraits of Jehanne la Pucelle and her husband Robert des Armoises. Their coat of arms are also in the salon.

THE REAL
JOAN OF ARC?

Nora Wooster

The Book Guild Ltd.
Sussex, England.

The Book Guild Ltd.
25 High Street,
Lewes, Sussex.

First published 1992
© Nora Wooster 1992
Set in Baskerville
Typesetting by Southern Reproductions (Sussex)
East Grinstead, Sussex.
Printed in Great Britain by
Antony Rowe Ltd.
Chippenham, Wiltshire.

A catalogue record for this book
is available from the British Library.

ISBN 0 86332 676 5

The Church has nothing to gain by spreading vain legends, and nothing to lose by the manifestation of historical truth.

Pope Pius XII

CONTENTS

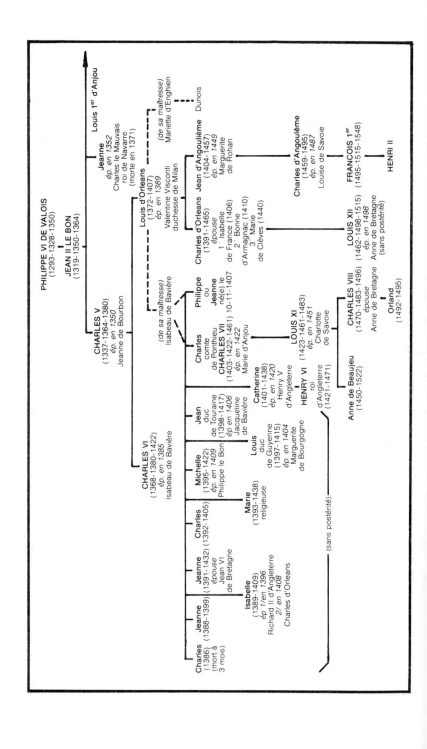

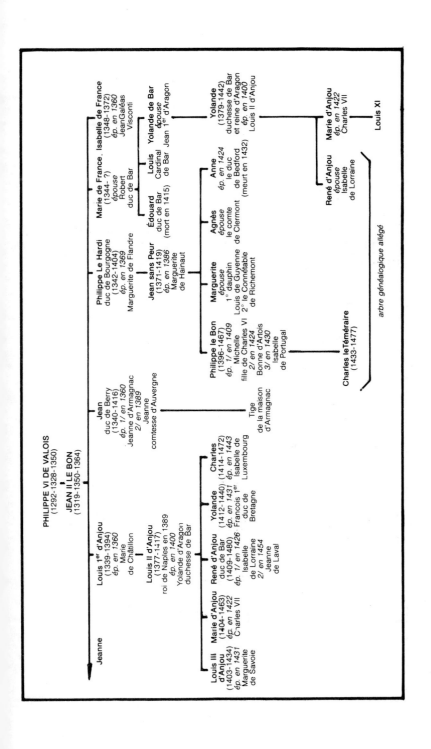

PHILIPPE VI DE VALOIS
(1292-1328-1350)

JEAN II LE BON
(1319-1350-1364)

Jeanne

Louis 1er d'Anjou
(1339-1394)
ép. en 1360
Marie
de Châtillon

Louis II d'Anjou
(1377-1417)
roi de Naples en 1389
ép. en 1400
Yolande d'Aragon
duchesse de Bar

Marie d'Anjou
(1404-1463)
ép. en 1422
Charles VII

René d'Anjou
duc de Bar
(1409-1480)
ép. 1/ en 1426
Isabelle
de Lorraine
2/ en 1454
Jeanne
de Laval

Yolande
(1412-1440)
ép. en 1431
Francois 1er
duc de
Bretagne

Charles
(1414-1472)
ép. en 1443
Isabelle de
Luxembourg

Louis III
d'Anjou
(1403-1434)
ép. en 1431
Marguerite
de Savoie

Jean
duc de Berry
(1340-1416)
ép. 1/ en 1360
Jeanne d'Armagnac
2/ en 1389
Jeanne
comtesse d'Auvergne

Tige
de la maison
d'Armagnac

Philippe Le Hardi
duc de Bourgogne
(1342-1404)
ép. en 1369
Marguerite de Flandre

Jean sans Peur
(1371-1419)
ép. en 1386
Marguerite
de Hainaut

Philippe le Bon
(1396-1467)
ép. 1/ en 1409
Michelle
fille de Charles VI
2/ en 1424
Bonne d'Artois
3/ en 1430
Isabelle
de Portugal

Charles le Téméraire
(1433-1477)

Marguerite
épouse
1° dauphin
Louis de Guyenne
2° le Connétable
de Richemont

Agnès
épouse
le comte
de Clermont

Anne
ép. en 1424
le duc
de Bedford
(meurt en 1432)

Marie de France, Isabelle de France
(1344- ?)   (1348-1372)
épouse   ép. en 1360
Robert   JeanGaléas
duc de Bar   Visconti

Édouard
duc de Bar
(mort en 1415)

Louis
Cardinal
de Bar

Yolande de Bar
épouse
Jean 1er d'Aragon

Yolande
(1379-1442)
duchesse de Bar
et reine d'Aragon
ép. en 1400
Louis II d'Anjou

René d'Anjou
épouse
Isabelle
de Lorraine

Marie d'Anjou
ép. en 1422
Charles VII

Louis XI

arbre généalogique allégé

ACKNOWLEDGEMENT

The author, Nora Wooster together with The Book Guild, wish to express sincere gratitude to the following people and organisations for permission to reproduce photographs.

Editions Robert Laffont, Paris,
Jean-Jacques Pauvert, Editeur,
Editions Balzac,
Bernard Jean Daulon,
Editions La Baule,
La Pensée Universelle, Paris 4.

INTRODUCTION

Some twelve years ago whilst attending a Diamond Conference in Bristol University I heard that the 'facts' we had been taught about Joan of Arc - that she was an illiterate peasant girl who heard voices from Heaven whilst watching her father's sheep - was no more than a myth. Later investigation in Cambridge convinced me that the shepherdess was indeed the adulterine daughter of Isabeau of Bavaria Queen of France, and that the king's younger brother, Louis Duke of Orleans, was her father.

Discovering that many reputable French historians had spent much of their lives searching for what they believed to be the truth about Joan, I set out to acquire such of their books as I was able to find. Many were quite unobtainable because their authors had discovered not only was it difficult to get their work published, but even when they succeeded, their books were liable to be bought only to be destroyed, so determined were powerful vested interests to keep the truth hidden.

I am not a historian but a crystallographer, and I suppose I have written this book much as I would write a scientific paper. I have tried to give a straightforward chronological account of her life, and described the contemporary society, as I imagine most of my readers will know no more about fifteenth century conditions in France than I did myself when I began to read up this subject. Since we are English, most of Joan's contemporaries are unknown to us, but in order to indicate that I am writing about real people, I generally do give their names. But as there are so many they are apt to become confusing - so at the end of the book there is a glossary giving first a list of Joan's numerous relatives who

11

proved to be important to her, and then another of those other people who played an influential part in her life. Names not included in the glossary are unimportant! I have found that very many people are astonished to learn that the story of Joan of Arc is largely untrue and they are glad to hear the real facts. They are surprised, too, that a myth deliberately disseminated in the fifteenth century in order to mislead people, should still be supported by the French Government and the Vatican. Hundreds of books have been published about the mythical Joan, but relatively few concerning the real person who, interestingly enough, was never called Joan of Arc in her lifetime, but Joan the Maid – *Jehanne la Pucelle*. So far from being unlettered she was well educated, and signed her many letters 'Jehanne' or 'Jehanne la Pucelle'. For this reason I so-call her throughout my book. and correctly or not I pronounce her name as a single syllable to rhyme with Anne.

It is just as well now that we are in the Common Market to let French people know that we did NOT burn Jehanne but rescued her at the last moment from the French Inquisitional Court that had condemned her as a heretic and witch to be burned at the stake. To this end Pierre Cauchon the Bishop of Beauvais, who was the English Regent's chaplain, had striven to be appointed her judge to protect her! A 'real' witch was presumably burned in her stead – there were five available at the time. No record of Jehanne being burned is to be found in any of Rouen's archives nor any execution at all on that day.

Some years after her 'execution' she reappeared in Lorraine which then belonged to the Holy Roman Empire. Six months later she married a French aristocrat, Robert des Armoises. The marriage was childless. Jehanne died when she was forty-two years old and was buried in a little church whose construction she had helped to finance. It is in a small town called Pulligny-sur-Madon, not far from Nancy. A century later the descendants of Jehanne's godson, noticing that the tombstone was becoming defaced by the feet of the faithful, put a plaque on the nearby wall to draw attention to it. In 1890 when moves to beatify Joan of Arc were taking place, iconoclasts covered the tomb with kitchen tiles, and tore down the plaque.

A society still mainly feudal existed in France in the fifteenth century, and to understand why things happened as they did, I had a lot to learn: the importance of the mystique of royalty, the rigid distinctions between the classes, the enormous influence of the Church and the bitter feuds within it, the superstitious beliefs and the credulity of the people at large, the danger of assassination, the absence of any policing and much else – all this made a wholly different environment to that in which we live today.

I have tried to present the reader with a credible biography of Jehanne which could account for her exceptional personality and achievements. It faithfully incorporates the odd collection of established facts concerning her which have been unearthed by my 'dissident' historians. They have been equipped with the necessary skills and opportunities which I do not pretend to possess. A great deal about Jehanne is still unknown so I have adopted what seem to me reasonable suggestions concerning her, including that put forward in the periodical *History Today* 1958 by the Emeritus Professor of Physic in Cambridge and his wife, which account for her visions. They suggest that she experienced hallucinations.

I have striven all the time to make clear what the reader should regard as established fact as distinct from my suppositions. I think I have contributed the first reasonable explanation of why Jehanne was invited to visit the Duke of Lorraine's Court in Nancy before she was introduced to the French Court, and as a result managed to remove Charles's misgivings over his illegitimacy and doubtful right to the throne.

I gather that what I have written is in no sense what historians regard as HISTORY. Consequently it may be inadvisable for them to read my book, but I would be glad if it stimulated them seriously to study the subject themselves. The numbers in brackets occasionally found in the text refer to the 'Notes' which follow my 'Bibliography'. They provide information which I expect to interest my ordinary readers. Historians looking for information to substantiate the 'established facts' on which this 'biography' is based are referred to the extensive references to be found in the books named in my Bibliography.

Where my dissident sources disagree with one another, for

13

instance – was Jehanne really a visionary or did she seek to protect friends who were giving her advice by referring to them as Saints or Voices – I have always taken the line that Jehanne really believed that she was simply telling the truth. I am sure that she honestly considered that she frequently participated in a transcendental experience, and that at least once (in Poitiers) that other people had also experienced one at the same time as herself. I think it was an entirely reasonable interpretation on her part. She was some thirteen-and-a-half years old when she had her first hallucination, and from that time on, at least for many years, she experienced them with increasing frequency.

In the fifteenth century the New Year began at Easter, so that January 1440 would have been towards the end of the year, and the following May near the beginning of 1441. I have adopted the usual practice of converting all dates to begin at January 1st.

I am greatly indebted to my friends Mme Jeanne Bernon and Mme Colette Collignon (who owns the castle where Jehanne had lived with her husband) for having made it possible for me to get access to or acquire many of the works of the French authors mentioned in my Bibliography. Without their help and generosity I could not have contemplated writing about Jehanne la Pucelle.

1

Origin of Jehanne

Jehanne la Pucelle – as Joan of Arc was called when she was alive and famous – was born halfway though the Hundred Years War, in 1407. At that time a large part of the French kingdom had fallen into the hands of the English, and the remnant was the victim of internecine strife, stemming originally from a disastrous decision of a former French king, Jean le Bon. When he died he left the dukedom of Anjou to one son, Burgundy to another and Berry to a third. Previously all the territories reverted to the Crown when the monarch died, the incumbent receiving it back after acknowledging his feudal status and loyalty to the new king. But now Burgundy had taken advantage of its independence and was virtually a state within a state.

Charles VI 1380-1426
'The Well-Beloved'

The reigning king when Jehanne came into the world was Charles VI. He was a Valois. His father, Charles V, had died in 1380 when Charles was twelve years old and for some years a regency governed the country. The regents were the boy's

15

uncles, and they soon quarrelled among themselves and the treasury emptied. When Charles was seventeen his uncle the Duke of Burgundy suggested he should marry a German princess, Isabeau of Bavaria, because he held the mistaken idea that her family would provide an ally against the English. When Charles was shown her portrait he could hardly wait for the seductive and precocious black-haired fourteen-year-old to arrive. They fell passionately in love in spite of the diplomatic origin of the union.

Before long Charles managed to rid himself of his regents and intelligently invoked the help of the 'Marmousets', able members of the bourgeoisie, to help him govern the country. His real reign thus began full of promise, and he was nicknamed 'The Well-Beloved'. Isabeau soon had her first child, and then her second, both of whom died very young, but by 1392 she had three healthy offspring.

That summer an attempt was made to assassinate Charles's Constable – the head of his army – so he mounted an expedition to deal with the malefactor. On the way back to Paris, as they were going through the Forest of le Mans, Charles suddenly became raving mad, thought that he was surrounded by enemies, drew his sword and hacked about him. Some of his companions were killed and others wounded before he was overpowered. He was tied to a litter and brought home. The poor man was a victim of porphyria.[1] Some weeks later he apparently recovered, but the illness was intermittent. He had lucid intervals when he behaved normally, only to suffer another attack, but as time passed he became more and more lethargic, and less able to deal with his affairs at any time.

A new regency came into being – the king's uncle the Duke of Berry, the king's brother Louis Duke of Orleans, and his cousin Jean sans Peur (John the Fearless) Duke of Burgundy. Louis was a handsome young man, profligate, very attractive to women, a superb horseman, cultivated, highly intelligent, and with a ready wit. Jean lacked his cousin's good looks and graces. He was completely unscrupulous and also very able. They were deadly rivals, equally ambitious, and both had designs on the throne.

When the king was mad he developed an alarming hatred of

the queen, chasing her with a dagger if he caught sight of her. It became essential to find somewhere else for her to live until his sanity returned. She bought an opulent mansion, the Hotel Barbette, not far from St Pol where the king lived. Here the Duke of Orleans could easily keep her up to date with affairs of state, and she could keep up her spirits by entertaining her friends. She returned to St Pol when the king recovered his senses. For some years they continued intermittently to live a normal married life, and Isabeau produced five more children, but after 1405 she did not sleep with the king again. He had lost interest in her, having found, with the help of the Duchess of Anjou, a more agreeable and sympathetic mistress, Ovette de Champsdivers. But long before this, scandalous stories began to circulate about Isabeau's wild parties at the Hotel Barbette and her equally scandalous relations with Louis. When her son Charles arrived in 1403 plenty of people speculated about who his father might be. Like her other children he was born in a royal palace – St Pol – and although the king was lucid at the time, he did not question the child's paternity. He may well have known that according to Roman law he was legally the father of any child his wife might have. He could have bastards, she could not.

Affairs became unpleasantly complicated however when Isabeau discovered in 1407 that she was pregnant again. This time it would be absolutely certain that the king was not this child's father. Indeed she had not set eyes on the king for two years. It was equally certain that the father was Louis, Duke of Orleans.

Isabeau did not merely stand to lose her reputation, such as it was, but she was actually in real danger of losing her liberty by having another child. Queen Elena who had transgressed in this way finished up spending the rest of her life in a convent, a prospect that did not appeal to Isabeau in the least. The solution that had been found acceptable for Louis's last illegitimate baby, whose mother had died in childbirth – the willing adoption by his devoted and long-suffering wife – offered no way out. Even though it is probable that Isabeau's pregnancy was not widely known – she had put on a good deal of weight, the fashions of the time would have tended to disguise any bulge, and the fact that she had had so many babies already could well have ruined her figure – it was clearly of paramount importance that any baby she produced should disappear from view the moment that it arrived.

It is my firm belief that in this quandary Louis consulted Yolande, Duchess of Anjou. Yolande was the daughter of the king of Aragon and his French queen the Duchess of Bar. From an early age Yolande had shown herself to be a remarkable young woman. At the age of eleven she had refused to be affianced in the usual way, saying that she wanted to be old enough to judge for herself who would be a suitable husband. She consented to marry the Duke of Anjou when she was twenty-one. Yolande inherited her mother's duchy. Bar was a province on the eastern border of France. It was separated from Lorraine – which belonged to the Holy Roman Empire – by the river Meuse. Yolande's husband in addition to being Louis II of Anjou, was King of Naples and Sicily, King of Jerusalem, and Count of Provence. It was a happy marriage and they had five children. She was described as the handsomest woman in Christendom, was resourceful and full of initiative. It would be typical of Yolande to suggest that as soon as Isabeau had begun labour a newly dead baby should be smuggled into the hotel, and that when Isabeau's baby had arrived an announcement should be made that it had unfortunately died shortly after being christened. Then the corpse should be put in a small coffin and without delay taken with due pomp and ceremony to St Denis for interment with its royal ancestors. As quickly as possible after the new baby was christened it should be taken to a wet nurse who would look after it in some prearranged suitable place where it could be kept until it was possible to take it to foster parents. The wet nurse should not be aware of its parentage. Yes, Yolande would assure Louis, she would be able to find very suitable foster parents, and she would ask a good friend of hers to find them in good time.

Being a Valois Yolande's sympathies were naturally with Orleans rather than with Burgundy. Nevertheless the Anjou's policy was to build up alliances and understandings wherever possible, and with this in mind they had affianced their small boy Louis to Burgundy's four-year-old daughter Catherine. As was the custom amongst the aristocracy in those days, one

Yolande, Duchess of Anjou

19

of the affianced children came to live in the other's family, and Catherine had arrived with her dowry – tapestries, furniture, jewels, silver and gold, her wardrobe and a retinue of servants – to live with her future in-laws. The children grew up together, knowing that they were destined to marry when they were old enough.

There was another remarkable woman in France at that time – called Colette de Corbie. She was the daughter of an artisan and became a religious recluse. She had many intense religious experiences, and following one when she was twenty-five years old, became convinced that she should renounce her vows to be a recluse in order to reform the Franciscan sisterhood. It was no small matter to renounce one's vows, but in her case it proved surprisingly easy. When she was brought before Pope Benedict XIII he prostrated himself before her as soon as she entered the room, so impressed was he by her holiness and spirituality. Considering her reclusion to have been the equivalent of a novitiate he immediately had her dressed in the habit of a Clare sister and said, 'I allow you to call yourself Lady, Mother or Abbess as you wish for the whole of the reformation.'

He then conferred on her extensive powers to enable her to carry it out. It was typical of her that she always referred to herself as Sister Colette. 'Mother? . . . Abbess?' she is said to have exclaimed, 'Never!'

She quickly brought about a remarkable change in the order of the Poor Clares. 'She fused together by love women of all classes of society.' The wonderful reputation of her first establishment, not far from Poligny, led to the foundation of many others. She made her headquarters in a convent in Besançon.

One point in the rules of the Clares puzzled Colette. 'Say the divine office *en haut et sans chanter*' (with the voice raised but without singing). She asked her confessor Piérre Henri what it meant, but he could not help her. So they both knelt and asked the Lord what it meant and suddenly, according to a Sister Perrine who was in the room, 'A most melodious voice which seemed angelic rather than human showed them how to recite it.'

Colette was at once able to reproduce it admirably. It is known as *le ton céleste*.

Colette also had a profound influence on the Third Order of Saint Francis. This was a widespread movement which embraced the laity, particularly the women, who would meet regularly on a Saturday afternoon. People dedicated themselves to a mitigated form of religious rule. Among the many great ladies who were members were the Duchess of Burgundy and her three daughters. At the head of the organisation was Yolande, the Duchess of Anjou. She and Colette were close friends.

When Yolande considered the problem put to her by Louis, I suppose she decided without hesitation to dispatch the expected infant to the Bar. It was a long way from Paris and although it was bordered by English and Burgundian territory, not so long since King Charles V had bought a large estate from the Bourlement family who owned a castle in the village of Domremy, and the villagers had been raised to the status of Burgesses of the King. It was part of the 'Royal Domain' by his ordnance, and thus due to be protected by the castle at Vaucouleurs. So the loyalty of the district was not in question – though of course the parentage of the newcomer would not be generally disclosed. Colette de Corbie had a great deal of influence in that neighbourhood where the Third Order flourished. The ladies usually met on Saturday afternoons at the Hermitage of Bermont, half a league from Domremy. And that was where Colette always stayed when she was in that district.

There is an interesting and curious entry that summer in the accounts of the Hotel St Pol: 'On June 12th, 1407 a village woman called Jehanne Darc came to St Pol with garlands to offer the King Charles VI, for which she received recompense of eighteen sols.' This is the first time the name Jehanne Darc appears in any official record. One wonders if she expected to find Isabeau there and had provided the garlands in order to give herself an excuse to enter the palace without exciting suspicion. Her real object in travelling to Paris was doubtless to be introduced to Isabeau.

I expect when they did meet they discussed, amongst much else, when Jehanne should take up residence at the Hotel Barbette, and how she was to account for her being there. As she is referred to later as a lady-in-waiting we may suppose

21

that this was agreed upon then.

One can imagine how shocked Jehanne was at that court life, and how sincerely she would believe the child would be fortunate to be brought up in Domremy by her sister-in-law instead of staying with its mother. But be that as it may, she was in Barbette in November 1407 when Isabeau took to her bed to have as nearly clandestine a confinement as any French queen has ever had.[2]

I know of no clear account of the confinement, but at the Abbey of St Denis a record, the *Chroniques,* was kept by the monks of events concerning the Court.

> 'The evening of Saint Martin in Winter, towards two hours after midnight the august queen of France was delivered of a son at her mansion near the Barbette Gate. This infant scarcely lived, the attendants only having time to give him the name Philippe and baptise him in the name of the Saint and the Indivisible Trinity. The following evening the masters of the Court conveyed his body to the Abbey of Saint Denis with many torches, according to custom, and consigned him with his brothers in the chapel of the king his ancestor.'

This is the sole contemporary mention of Philippe. His birth was not registered at Saint-Germaine d'Auxerrois, the king's parish. (There is no mention of Jehanne's birth either here or in Domremy).

Actually the queen gave birth to a baby girl, who was christened Jehanne, either by her father or a Celestine monk, for Louis was the great protector of that order, and doubtless Jehanne Darc was her godmother. Her birth may be said to have been acknowledged in 1770 when a new edition of the official History of France was published by a reputable historian, M. Villaret. On page 305 of Volume VII the name of Isabeau's last child is named Jeanne (sic), instead of Philippe, given on page 169 of Volume XIV, published in 1763.

The queen was said to be deeply distressed by the loss of Philippe and was in tears for the next twelve days. But it is my belief that she shared the anxiety felt by the king's uncle. For some months the Duke of Berry had been greatly alarmed by

22

the bitter enmity displayed by his two nephews. Louis missed no opportunity of publicly ridiculing his cousin, who was incapable either of ignoring it or of replying in kind. Breaking point had been reached when Louis thought it would be very amusing to record Jean sans Peur's reaction at seeing his wife's portrait displayed in Louis's picture gallery of the many ladies he had successfully seduced. Nobody, least of all Louis, expected anyone to take the libel seriously, for the Duchess's reputation was spotless. But Jean had stormed out of the building, vowing that he would exterminate the whole House of Orleans. His uncle at least took the threat quite literally. I think it very probable that Isabeau was equally worried that Burgundy might kill her as well as Louis. And yet though she had lamented almost without ceasing for twelve days, she suddenly cheered up on the thirteenth day and announced that she was going to have a Joyous Supper in her bedroom that evening. It has been suggested that this was because the baby girl had been safely sent on her way to Domremy. However, the weather was so atrocious I cannot believe it. One of the severest frosts on record occurred that year and lasted thirty-six days without remission. The Seine was frozen over. The idea of travelling in such weather with a very young baby over hundreds of miles would have been out of the question. But on that very day Louis would have been able to assure Isabeau that the danger from Burgundy was over.

On November 20, a Sunday, the Duke of Berry had tricked his two nephews into meeting him and each other in an Augustinian chapel where they solemnly swore to be reunited. They attended mass together and then both partook of Holy Communion. This solemn ceremony was followed by a grand banquet at the Hotel de Nesle where they again confirmed their unbreakable friendship. They signed an act of confraternity, mutually accepted the order of chivalry and separated with a thousand protestations that from now on there should be complete understanding between them. Two days later they renewed their vows in the presence of the king and Court, who showed singular kindness. They took bread and drank wine together. Louis invited Jean sans Peur to dine with him the following Sunday, and the invitation was accepted. They embraced each other on leaving. Surely this reconciliation was worth a celebration?

Jean sans Peur, Duke of Burgundy 1371-1419

Isabeau's brother Louis of Bavaria was among the guests at the Joyous Supper. Louis her beloved arrived incognito on a mule with a couple of equerries sharing a horse and a few servants came on foot. The party was going well when there was a knock on the door. A servant stood there. He had brought a message from the king who asked Louis to return to St Pol at once as he wished to discuss something of great interest to both of them. Louis left immediately with his small escort, only to run into an ambush of eighteen armed men at the next corner.

The equerries' horse bolted at the sight of them, and Louis was left alone.

'I am the Duke of Orleans,' he said, supposing they had made a mistake.

'So much the better, it is you we want,' was the reply.

Someone severed his hand holding the bridle, he was knocked off his mule by a mace and his skull crushed by a club bristling with iron spikes. One servant coming up and trying to defend his master was killed. The others dashed back to Barbette with the terrible news. Isabeau, terrified and grief-stricken, was taken by her brother to St Pol at once, and installed in the chamber next to the king's.

Burgundy pretended the following day to be as shocked and horrified as everyone else. He even acted as pall-bearer at Louis's funeral, but someone living in a house in the street where the murder had taken place recognized one of the assassins, and he was traced to Burgundy's palace. When Jean discovered that he was seriously suspected his nerve gave way and he actually admitted his guilt. He immediately fled to his most distant residence – a castle in Flanders. He wrecked the bridge at Saint Maxence on the way in order to delay pursuit, but in fact no-one followed him.

When Louis's murderer was identified the Duke and Duchess of Anjou sent Catherine and her trousseau and retainers back to her parents, without a word of explanation.

2

The Darc Family

I believe Colette chose a family called Darc to foster the new baby. They belonged to a long-established minor noble

Original Darc Coat of Arms

family who had borne a coat of arms for over two centuries and could boast several distinguished ancestors. In 1331 Jean Darc was appointed bishop of Mende, and later he was made bishop of Langres. In 1375, Marie Darc had married the then Duke of Burgundy; Simon Darc was chaplain of Notre Dame in the king's chateau of Chaumont de Bassigny and Pierre Darc was a canon at Troyes. As their name indicated they had originated in the village of Arc-en-Barrois. The apostrophe in d'Arc was not introduced until the sixteenth century.

When Jehanne was brought to Domremy, the head of the family was Jacques Darc. He had been born in Ceffonds in Champagne about 1375. The family coat of arms is carved in stone in the church there.[3a] His family's estates had been devastated during the early years of the Hundred Years War, and the Black Death which ravaged France during 1334 had impoverished the family still further.

Jacques decided to derogate in 1400. This meant that he renounced his noble status in order to be allowed to work. Derogation did not necessarily become permanent, should he prosper sufficiently and retain his good reputation he could have his noble status restored, and in fact this happened to him later.

Selling up the remains of his possessions in Ceffonds he moved to Domremy and leased twenty hectares of arable and pasture land, and became a successful breeder of cattle. His wife, Isabelle de Vouton, whose family had been ruined in the same way, added some hectares of forest to their holding by her dowry. She was normally called Isabelle Romée because some ancestress had made a pilgrimage to Rome.[3b]

Domremy at that time was a village with some thirty households. The Darcs were comfortably off and lived in quite the best house in the village, with six large living rooms, at once farmhouse and manor. This no longer exists. Jacques cut a highly respected figure in the district, representing them as doyen, willingly undertaking responsibilities and accepting honours. He was a supporter of the House of Orleans, and his wife who came from a deeply religious family, was an enthusiastic member of the Third Order of Saint Francis. They had two children at this time, a boy and a girl.

There was a castle in the village near the church owned by the Bourlemont family which offered shelter to the villagers and their livestock if they were threatened by bandits or marauding soldiers.

It does seem that the secret of Jehanne's existence was successfully kept at that time. When the weather permitted, a party of some ten people including a wet nurse and Jehanne Darc, set out with the baby for Domremy – some say on horseback, while others provide a carriage. They arrived in the middle of the night of January 6th. An amusing description of it has survived in a letter written to Philippe Visconti, Duke of Milan. He was the brother of Louis d'Orleans's widow. The writer was Percival de Boulainvilliers, later a chamberlain of Charles VII.

'On the 6th of January in the night of Epiphany, the cocks began to crow. Men carrying torches had disturbed the habitual quiet. They knocked on the door of the doyen Jacques Darc. And the villagers, unaware of the birth of Jehanne, came to find out what the fuss was about.'

One suspects that the travellers were hungry and glad to enjoy some freshly roasted chicken. It is past belief that any villager supposed the new addition to the Darc family was Isabelle's own. It would be assumed that the baby was some aristocrat's embarrassment, but it is most unlikely that anyone supposed she was a royal princess. I doubt if even Jacques himself knew this. Her (second!) christening took place a week later in Domremy's church with an unprecedented number of godparents – four godfathers and five godmothers were provided for the eight week old newcomer.

There is not much evidence concerning Jehanne's early childhood. It seems she was brought up in just the same way as the other Darc children. She called Isabelle and Jacques mother and father. One does not know if as a child she knew she was adopted, but hints had probably been dropped by servants and villagers even if she had not been told, and she may well have wondered why she looked so unlike the rest of the family. She played with her contemporaries in the village and made good friends amongst them. Probably she grew up trilingual – speaking French at home, the French patois of the village and the largely German language of the peasants in Lorraine. She attended school at the nearby village of Maxey, where she learned to read and write. Isabelle taught her her prayers and how to sew and spin. She did not look after her father's cattle nor his sheep.

A Franciscan Tertiary, Bessonet-Favre, who wrote a book about Jehanne, quotes a local legend which was current in the Bar countryside that Saint Colette de Corbie left a mysterious ring on Jehanne's bed in 1412. This ring had been given to Colette by St John the Evangelist when he had appeared to her once, as a pledge of the mystical union she was contracting with Jesus. It was inscribed with the words Jhesus-Maria and three crosses with equal length arms in a circle. This was the symbol of the Third Order. That same year in August Isabelle Romée was warned that 'The Lord had particular and mysterious prospects for this blessed child.' As a member of the Third Order she would have understood this to mean that Jehanne was destined to become a Poor Clare. To take the veil was the normal fate for girls who were obliged to keep their origin secret. Isabelle and her brother who was the vicar of Sermaize doubtless did their best to prepare the little girl for such a life. Jehanne certainly responded with a deep religious faith and sincere wish to help those less fortunate than herself.

Domremy, although a small place, was not isolated nor without some commercial importance. The Meuse supported a lively traffic in ships going north carrying Burgundian wine and returning with Flanders woollen cloth and manufactures. The village was on the old Roman road joining Verdun and Langres and many travellers made use of it, great lords and merchants, troubadours and scholars, artisans and monks and not least the Mendicant Friars. Many would have availed themselves of the Darc's hospitality and regaled their hosts with travellers' tales and the latest news.

It is interesting to note that after Jehanne was installed in the Darc family a number of their relatives received notable appointments. Guillaume Darc became a King's Counsellor, and was made tutor to the then dauphin Louis, Duke of Guyenne; Raoul Darc was appointed the king's chamberlain, and later became a seneschal in Aveyron; in 1409 Yvon Darc was made bailiff, and later became the dauphin's Counsellor.

The owner of the Bourlemont castle dying childless, he bequeathed it to his great-niece Jehanne de Joinville. She married Jehan d'Ogiviller who came from Lorraine. They lived in the castle for some years then moved to the Lorraine Court in Nancy, leaving the place uninhabited. It was an increasingly lawless time with bands of one-time soldiers and mercenaries little better than brigands roaming the country-side. They were liable to go on pillaging forays and the Burgundians to the south were not to be trusted if an opportunity to make trouble occurred. In 1419 Jacques Darc and another man in the village took out a lease on the castle for nine years from the Lady Ogiviller and the Darcs moved from their thatched house to the castle whose stout outer defensive walls enclosed a large garden.[4]

3

Political Background

Although Valentine de Milan, Louis d'Orleans's widow, did her best to have Jean sans Peur punished for her husband's murder she failed completely, and so far from losing all influence he managed in the following year to be reinstated in the king's good graces. He paid an eminent theologian in the Sorbonne to plead his case, and after making inordinately long speeches on Burgundy's behalf, he extracted a pardon from Charles VI for murdering Louis on the grounds that he had been a tyrant who deserved to be put to death!

Louis of Orleans was succeeded by his son Charles who shortly afterwards married Bonne d'Armagnac. His father-in-law was an eminent soldier who was prepared to fight on his behalf, and before long the country was in a state of civil war. This only had the effect of devastating the countryside, ruining trade, and encouraging the English to renew hostilities in support of their claims to the French throne.

The Anjous noted with some alarm ties developing between Burgundy and the royal family. The dauphin Louis was affianced to and then married Burgundy's daughter Marguerite. His younger brother Jean Duke of Touraine married the queen's cousin who was the daughter of one of Burgundy's vassals. In an effort to strengthen their ties with the Valois, Yolande proposed affiancing the queen's youngest son Charles, Count of Pontieu, to her little daughter Marie. Isabeau accepted this suggestion with enthusiasm; she was glad to be rid of her unprepossessing (and could be embarrassing) child. He was an ugly, unattractive little boy, pale, puny and knock-kneed – even his eyes were of different colour. It is said that she had earlier remarked to her brother that she did not care whom the child married, if indeed anyone would have him!

At least the betrothal would afford an opportunity for a splendid party, which was arranged in 1413 to celebrate their engagement. Isabeau gave expensive presents to all concerned. Yolande took Charles home with her to Provence, and a genuinely affectionate relationship developed between them. He called her his *Bonne Mère.* He was an intelligent ten-year-old. Charles then experienced the first happy period of his life. Nine years later their marriage was solemnised. They must have made a pathetic little couple – Marie had inherited none of her mother's good looks. Indeed she was said to be ugly enough to frighten the English, and he was still an undersized and ugly weakling.

Soon after the death of our Henry IV in 1413, Henry V began collecting funds to enable him to invade France. He began with a spectacular success in early 1415 by capturing Harfleur and destroying the French fleet, and then a few months later continued to triumph with the overwhelming victory of Agincourt, when 10,000 French cavaliers were killed. In addition not a few notables, including the Duke of Orleans, his brother and the Duke of Bourbon, were taken prisoner and held to ransom. The sum demanded for Orleans was so exorbitant that he remained exiled in London for twenty-five years, though the fact that he seemed to be enjoying his existence there, writing delightful lyrical poems, may have had some influence on the length of his stay. The diminution of power and impoverishment of the French party through Agincourt can hardly be overestimated.

Henry was unable to follow up his successful victories for lack of funds. But though hostilities had ceased the deterioration of France's position continued. In 1416 when Jean sans Peur learned of an alliance of mutual help signed by the Holy Roman Emperor Sigismund and Henry V, Jean decided to do likewise, considering that this would be the simplest way to get rid of the Valois line. Towards the end of the year he signed the Pact of Calais, allying himself to Henry and acknowledging that he was the rightful king of France. He gladly promised to help him oust Charles VI. Doubtless with this promise in mind, the following year the Burgundians murdered the dauphin Louis Duke of Guyenne by poison, even though he was married to Marguerite of Burgundy.

By this time Henry had managed to collect more funds and men so he was able to renew hostilities which had been in abeyance since Agincourt. Meanwhile the civil war had continued with undiminished ferocity. Even a reconciliation within the Church led to a reduction in the French king's support, for the pope Benedict XIII in Avignon acknowledged Martin V in Rome as head of the Roman Catholic Church, and Martin favoured the English king. Though the French king's friend Benedict continued to live in Avignon, his influence was greatly diminished.

On the death of his brother, Jean, Duke of Touraine became dauphin. But because he was a supporter of the Anglo-Burgundian alliance, he was poisoned by the Armagnacs, and found lying dead, his lips and tongue hideously bloated, his eyes starting from his head. This meant that Charles the king's only surviving son, became dauphin and heir to the throne. The Duke of Anjou was one of the regents at the time and he managed to get Charles VI to declare that he had delegated his royal powers to his son Charles, Count of Pontieu, in order to defend the kingdom. He styled him Lieutenant General.

Isabeau was now behaving with such outrageous promiscuity that Armagnac persuaded the king to have her sent to a convent in Monmoutier near Tours in January 1417. Her current lover Louis de Boisredan was sewn up in a sack and thrown into the Seine. Finding chastity insupportable, she managed with the help of Jean sans Peur (of all people!) to escape on November 2, 1417, and took refuge with him in his fortified castle at Troyes. There she announced that she was 'Queen of France by the Grace of God' and set up a simulacrum of government with Parlement, Chancellery and Treasury.

Isabeau, perhaps compelled by the Burgundians, then wrote to Yolande demanding that she send the dauphin Charles back to her. Yolande replied with a masterly letter:

'A woman provided with lovers has no need of children. I have not fed and brought him up so that he could be allowed to die like his brothers; or sent mad like his father; or sold to the English as you are.

I guard him as my own; come and take him if you dare!'

Isabeau of Bavaria
(contemporary portrait)

Louis II of Anjou fell ill and died on April 28, 1417. Yolande was thirty-seven years old. The safeguarding of her family's heritage was now her responsibility. When making his will Louis had exhorted his wife, children and son-in-law to adopt a policy of conciliation and cooperation in their affairs whenever possible. Yolande would have felt no difficulty in following her husband's advice to adopt peaceful means of getting her own way if at all feasible, and she managed to avoid military action most of the time.

The fact that her daughter Marie was affianced to Charles and could therefore expect to become queen, meant that Yolande was now as interested in maintaining the Valois dynasty as the rest of her family's heritage. She showed herself to be a wonderful organiser, possessed of enormous patience, aware that it can sometimes pay to retreat, prepared to use her own resources if they were the only present means available, and ready to pay herself back when circumstances had changed for the better. She had no urge to enrich herself at public expense. She was a shrewd though not infallible judge of character, and very willing deliberately to make use of others' frailties to her own advantage. She was quite exceptional in foreseeing contingencies which no one else was aware of, and had the energy and courage to make use of whatever circumstances or people were available in order to make apparently impossible situations actually occur.

By the end of 1417 not only Burgundy but many other princes were supporting the English. Jean IV of Brittany had a secret treaty with Henry, similar to Burgundy's. Charles le Hardi (the Bold) of Lorraine, married to a relative of Burgundy, was also a firm friend of the English and a fanatical enemy of Armagnac. Only the Duke of Savoy remained loyal to the Valois, but he could not be relied upon to take an active role. Orleans and Bourbon were still prisoners in England. While Armagnac was staunchly anti-Burgundian he and his followers had made themselves extremely unpopular in the countryside by pillaging mercilessly wherever they fought their battles.

Yolande came to the conclusion that it was essential to form a united front of French princes if the English were ever to be driven out of the country. She decided her first tentative move would be to make some use of Jean IV, Duke of Brittany.

Charles had become very sensitive about his questionable paternity. His enemies had made the most of this, and he was often referred to as the 'so-called dauphin'. He had developed a morbid fear that his physical disabilities were a consequence of his parents' guilt, which greatly contributed to his melancholy and diffidence. Nevertheless he was the sole heir to the throne since his two brothers had been eliminated, and anyway he could claim to have the blood of Saint Louis in his veins. Yolande was determined to endow him and the people of France with an unshakeable belief in his divine right to rule the kingdom.

She invited Jean IV to visit her in her castle at Angers where she had installed herself with Charles. She explained the visit was simply to introduce the future king to his illustrious vassal. Yolande coached Charles on how to behave. Supported by his Bonne Mère he lost his paralysing shyness and was charming and polite. He was endowed with an exceptionally pleasant voice, and Jean found him well informed and interesting to talk to. He and Yolande beguiled their visitor so completely that they all three signed the friendly Treaty of Angers. This was important to Yolande and Charles because it described him as 'Son of the king of France, dauphin of the Viennois, Duke of Touraine and of Berry, Count of Poitou, and Lieutenant General of the king.' It was valuable for the way it helped to consolidate the dauphin's legitimacy. To the same end Yolande was always punctilious in addressing Charles as befitted the heir apparent, both to enhance his self-esteem and to set an example to others of the correct way to behave towards him.

The Treaty of Angers was only a small step forward in Yolande's grandiose plan, but it was a beginning. Later she learned that the Duke of Brittany's brother Arthur de Richemont, who had been captured at Agincourt, when freed had given his services to the English. When he asked for promotion he had been laughed at for his pains. Yolande took advantage of this situation to propose her young daughter should be affianced to Jean's heir, and simultaneously offered to appoint Richemont, Charles's Constable of France. He was glad to accept, and for the first time she felt real confidence in the leader of her armed forces.

Yolande was well aware that many men past their prime find a certain rejuvenation in the intimate company of an attractive young woman, so she made it her business to find intelligent and charming French girls without substantial prospects, who were prepared to become someone's mistress in return for a much higher standard of living than they would otherwise have known. At the same time they would enjoy the honest belief that they were furthering the interests of their country. They would endeavour to bring about changes in the opinions and activities of their paramours to conform with those that Yolande wished them to hold. It was a stratagem that proved extraordinarily successful.

Yolande, for many reasons, wanted Lorraine to be added to the dauphin's allies. Charles the Bold had two daughters. The elder, Isabelle, was the apple of her father's eye, and he named her as his heir. When this was announced she became the most eligible young woman in Europe, and her hand was sought, amongst others, by Henry V and Louis of Bavaria, Isabeau's brother. Yolande approached the elderly cardinal Guillaume who was her uncle. He was the ruler of Bar, and she suggested he should make her second son René his heir. Guillaume was happy to oblige his charming niece and indeed it seemed a good choice as the boy inherited many of his mother's good qualities. Meanwhile, Charles the Bold had acquired a lively, devoted and very beautiful mistress, a French girl called Alison du May, who had already given the old man the first of five delightful youngsters. To the astonishment of nearly everyone, Charles offered his beloved daughter Isabelle to Cardinal Guillaume as a bride for his great nephew René d'Anjou. Charles the Bold had lost all interest in Henry's affairs. Indeed he hoped the French king would regain his territories. The young people were affianced on June 14, 1419 and they were married in 1426. It was a happy marriage.

Yolande then managed to arrange truces with Burgundy and England, signed by herself as well as the Lieutenant General, which while fragile brought about a small degree of stability. She decided her next priority must be Provence which Yolande had visited with her husband some years previously – a prosperous Provence of which she was the countess. But now she was hearing alarming reports of poverty and mismanagement there. She assembled a Council of wise men to look after the dauphin while she was away, and left with her two youngest children, Yolande and Charles. Typically she soon replaced chaos with order and encouraged the growth of the university at Aix which her husband had founded. Her eldest son Louis III returned from Italy for a while to add to his father's endowment, and it quickly attained the eminence it subsequently maintained. The dauphin visited her too and was received with pomp and ceremony. She stayed for a time in all the important towns, Aix, Arles, Tarascon and Avignon. The province became peaceful and prosperous again.

During this period there was one humane and unifying influence striving to counteract the greed and hatred that fuelled the civil war. The Third Order of St Francis was inspired by many of the ideals of the late lamented Knights Templar: a single sovereign for a united Christendom, the championship of the poor and feeble, and ultimately the rescue of Jerusalem from the Infidel. Yolande, politically on one side and the Duchess of Burgundy and her daughters on the other, were all actively working with each other to bring about the end of the civil war. Colette de Corbie and the Mendicant Friars, equally welcome in both camps, acted as advisors, coordinators and couriers for the Third Order. At last in 1419 the combatants were tentatively persuaded that the time had come to bury their hatchets unless they wished to see the English establish a stranglehold on the whole of France, which would ultimately benefit none of them. Even Jean sans Peur (who had acquired a new and charming mistress called Jeanne de Naillac, Dame de Giac), came to realize with her help that the economic links between his territories of Burgundy and Flanders might well be endangered if the English became complete masters of the intervening provinces. And Jean had been very riled when Henry boasted that he intended to 'marry the daughter of your king, with France as a dowry and apanage.'

After a preliminary talk engineered by Colette de Corbie which seemed to promise some kind of truce, a more formal meeting was arranged to take place at Montereau where Jean sans Peur would meet the dauphin and propose joint activities against the English. Extraordinary precautions were taken, for Jean sans Peur was very doubtful of the wisdom of his participation. 'By my faith, I know I risk my life. But if I return safe and sound, I shall take the people of my lord the Dauphin and together we shall fight.'

An excellent precis of what happened is given in David Hume's History of England, (Vol.III,p.85):

> 'The two princes came to Montereau: the duke lodged in the castle, the dauphin in the town, which was divided from the castle by the river Yonne: the bridge between them was chosen as the place of interview: two high rails were drawn across the bridge: the gates on each side were guarded, one by the officers of the dauphin, the other by those of the duke: the princes were to enter into the inter-mediate space by the opposite gates, accompanied each by ten persons; and with all these marks of diffidence to conciliate their mutual friendship; but it appears that no precautions are sufficient where laws have no place, and where all the principles of honour are utterly abandoned. Tanguy du Chatel and others of the dauphin's retainers had been zealous partisans of the late duke of Orleans: . . . They no sooner entered the rails than they drew

Philippe le Bon, Duke of Burgundy
1396-1467, son of Jean sans Peur.

their swords · and attacked the duke of Burgundy;
his friends were astonished and thought not of
making any defence; and all of them either shared
his fate or were taken prisoners by the retinue of the
dauphin.'

Whether the dauphin had expected the assassination to
take place is not known. I think it most unlikely. But the result
was, of course, to drive the Burgundians back into the arms of
the English. Philippe le Bon who inherited the dukedom in
December 1419 formally allied himself with the English as his
father had done. His contract lasted until 1435.

Yolande at this time was still in Provence with her children.
Had she not been, one cannot believe so gross a political error
would have been made. Indeed, in other ways too, the
absence of Yolande was sorely felt. The councillors she had left
to look after the dauphin made a mess of everything. Rivalries
developed between them. Louvet enriched himself at the
public expense, and he set out to undermine the dauphin's
faith in Robert de Maçon, whose integrity was hard to put up
with; Tanguy du Chatel while devoted, was incapable of
understanding Yolande's patient and persistent methods. It
was he who had organised the disastrous assassination of Jean
sans Peur, thus ruining the efforts of the Third Order and the
more subtle efforts of the Lady de Giac. The shameful Treaty
of Troyes was the direct result of the murder and all Yolande's
efforts of a peaceful solution were destroyed at a stroke.

On May 20th 1420, after acquiring Normandy and further conquests which included Rouen after a pitiless seige, Henry V and his brother the Duke of Clarence, with a derisory 1500 men, marched to Troyes with the agreed text of a treaty described as the most humiliating ever suffered by the French. It was signed the next day by Henry V and Charles VI. Poor Charles was too ill to have any idea what he was doing, he did not know who Henry was, and just did what Isabeau told him to do. For a long time she was paid a monthly pension of 2000 gold francs by the English to show their appreciation of her efforts.

The Treaty of Troyes agreed that Charles VI was to remain King of France until his death, and then the King of England was to become the King of France and England. Until then Henry was to keep Normandy as his own and receive the homage of the Duke of Brittany. He was given the hand of the King's daughter Catherine in marriage. The 'so-called dauphin' was disinherited for the reason that he was not the king's son, but a bastard. Henry, for his part, undertook to combine his army with Charles's and the Duke of Burgundy's and conquer all the territory held by the Armagnacs and Orleanists.

The marriage of Henry and Catherine took place twelve days later in Troyes. Enguerrard de Monstrelet the official Burgundian historian wrote:

> 'It was plainly to be seen that King Henry was desperately in love with her, while the black-haired Princess of France had longed passionately to be espoused to King Henry.'

Isabeau actually swore with her hand on the New Testament before Henry's brother the Duke of Bedford and Pierre Cauchon the deputy of the Archbishop of Rheims, that Charles's father was the Duke of Orleans. Unwilling as one might be to credit anything Isabeau swore to, there is good reason to believe that she was speaking the truth this time. Charles's birthday was February 23rd 1403. His conception would normally have been expected to occur in the second fortnight of May 1402, during which period Isabeau was living in Barbette. It is recorded that the king took part in a joust on

May 10th and 11th, when he could be presumed to be enjoying a lucid period. A crisis developed the following day or the day after. (One wonders if the weather had been hot and sunny[1].) He was ill for four weeks until June 10th. Thus to have been father to Charles VII, Isabeau's pregnancy must have lasted nine months and twelve days, or if she had conceived after June 10th, a maximum of eight months ten days. It would also imply that she had rushed back to St Pol the moment the king recovered, which was very unlikely, because when the king was ill he believed himself to be made of glass so would allow no one to wash him or change his clothes lest he should shatter into pieces. Consequently his body was covered with sores and vermin and 'suffused an odour that no one could put up with.'

On September 1st, after a further series of successful sieges Henry V, Philippe and Charles VI made a ceremonial entry into Paris. The English occupation lasted for fifteen years.

After a triumphal return to England and the coronation of the queen in Westminster Abbey, Henry returned to France and besieged more towns. It was a desperately cold and wet winter. Dysentery and smallpox broke out in his army and he fell ill with a fistula, from which he did not recover. He died in Vincennes, on August 31st 1422, aged thirty-five years.

Six weeks later Charles VI died. Henry's son born the previous December at Windsor Castle, was proclaimed King of England and France in England, and King of France and England in France. As Henry V had directed, the Regency was offered to Philippe but he declined it. The Duke of Bedford became the Regent in France. Shortly after he married Anne, Jean sans Peur's youngest daughter. His headquarters in France were in the Bouvreuil Castle in Rouen.

The 'so-called dauphin' was crowned at Poitiers as Charles VII of France. It was impossible for him to follow the tradition of being crowned in Rheims and anointed with the Holy Oil that had been sent from Heaven for Clovis's baptism. Rheims had been used for all but one French king's coronation since then, but both it and the abbey where the oil was kept were in English hands at that time.

Charles was seventeen when he heard that Charles VI had died. According to the Law of Heredity he had rightfully become king, and some of his supporters raised their swords

CHARLES VII.

Gravé d'après l'Original du Cabinet du Roi, par N.T.Maviez.

King Charles VII 1403-1461,
when young, by Maviez.

to him in acknowledgement. Charles simply hung his head and wept. Yolande was in Provence and he felt utterly alone and abandoned, quite unable to cope with the situation. In spite of the unremitting care and understanding, his Bonne Mère lavished upon him he so lacked any feeling of inner security he was incapable of making up his own mind upon any course of action. Yolande seemed to have accepted that it was not his fault that he was lacking in almost every characteristic one would like to find in an heir to the throne.

Certainly Charles had suffered far more than his fair share of horrifying experiences while he was young. He had been shaken awake in the middle of the night by Tanguy du Chatel to be rescued at the last moment from a crowd of rioters in Paris who massacred two thousand people. He was fourteen when he learned that his eldest brother Louis had been murdered, and then eighteen months later that his older brother Jean had been found poisoned as well. He was not merely present when Jean sans Peur was hacked to death on the bridge at Montereau, but so close that his clothes were bespattered by the victim's blood. This caused him to develop a phobia about meeting his own end in the same horrible way. Then in 1422 he was about to preside at a meeting of notables in La Rochelle, when the wooden floor of the hall they were in suddenly gave way, leaving him suspended whilst everyone else was hurled screaming into the void below. He was patently nervous of unfamiliar wooden structures ever after, hating to trust himself to a wooden bridge or staircase that he did not know. He couldn't bear to have strangers staring at him, and was often afflicted by a paralysing shyness, which left him without a word to say. Yet he was very intelligent, a good latinist, well versed in history, and had a remarkable memory. If he once felt at ease with a person he could be a charming companion and a good raconteur. He was very fond of his wife, and retained a tender affection for her. She had a retiring disposition, but always maintained her dignity. She probably understood him as well as her mother did. She gave him thirteen children.

Charles was horribly conscious of his miserable physique and ugly face. His nose was too big and his mouth loose and sensual, his eyes lack-lustre and shifty. Yet when he had the

Queen Marie of Anjou 1404-1463
wife of Charles VII

support of his Bonne Mère on state occasions, and she had rehearsed with him beforehand how he should behave, he managed to display an unforced princely air that could impress his audience very favourably.

As he grew up it was clear that he had inherited Isabeau's immoderate appetite for the opposite sex. This resulted in people who were willing and able to provide him with the means to gratify his craving, exerting undue influence over him. While Yolande was in Provence, Louvet whom she had appointed head of the dauphin's Council, made use of his pretty daughter in this way, and manipulated Charles and his finances for his own benefit. Another more disreputable favourite was a stable lad, called Pierre Frotier, whom Charles promoted to be head of his equerries. His new chamberlain was du Giac, who had been attached to the Burgundian court before Montereau, and whose wife had been Jean sans Peur's influential mistress. There is no reason to suppose she expected him to be murdered there, but her husband almost certainly did, and felt it advisable to join the dauphin's household after the assassination.

Things soon changed when his Bonne Mère returned to Bourges. Tanguy du Chatel was tactfully sent off to Provence, where he could enjoy the pleasant climate and was able to prosper on the revenue of some salt monopoly as long as he stayed there. She managed to remove several other undesirable friends of the king in like civilized manner. Yolande renewed her friendly contact with Brittany, which had lapsed while she had been absent. It was during this period that her younger daughter was affianced to Brittany's heir, and Jean VI's brother Arthur de Richemont was appointed Constable of France. Yolande began again to establish contact with Burgundy – there are records of payments made to a priest who delivered secret letters to him from her – always with the aim of detaching him from the English. But as Charles grew up there were times when he felt he must show his independence and would play truant with his favourites. And he developed an increasing hatred of Richemont.

4

L'Eminence Grise and God's Emissary

I am certain that Yolande would have fully appreciated how dangerously the Treaty of Troyes threatened all their futures: the extinction of the Valois line of kings, the confiscation of her family's and allies' lands in France, the very independence of France itself. No one but Yolande seemed capable of visualising, let alone organising, any effective resistance – though indeed, even with hindsight, when one considers what she was up against and the means at her disposal it must be agreed that the odds against success were all but insuper-able.

Obviously some charismatic leader was essential. Charles the dauphin, weedy, unprepossessing, lacking any firmness of purpose had none of the characteristics required. He was a liability rather than an asset. Dunois, Louis's bastard who had been adopted by his stepmother and brought up as though he had been her own son, had a military talent but lacked prestige. Charles, Duke of Orleans was likely to be detained in London *sine die* and anyway was far more adept at writing poetry than winning battles. The dauphin's cousin, the Duke of Alençon, was courageous but politically a lightweight, not in the right category as a leader. I believe Yolande realized that the only glimmer of hope came from that child in Domremy. She did show character and liveliness and was unusually intelligent. She was precocious, and Colette said that everyone who came into contact with her noticed her, and she was someone everybody liked. She alone seemed to have inherited the best traits of her ancestors. Clearly it was Jehanne or no one.

Jehanne would be thirteen in November. Granted that it

would be years before use could be made of her, equally those years could be profitably employed fitting her to cope with the problems she would be faced with when the time came to launch her. If she was to become a symbol of France able to enlist the enthusiasm of all kinds of people from the highest to the lowest, the countryside would have to be prepared to receive her. This was where the Third Order would prove its value, indeed the Franciscan Order generally. And Jehanne herself would certainly need years to be groomed for her exacting role.

There was a group of stalwarts Yolande could rely upon to discuss and help with such an undertaking. First and foremost was the irreplaceable Colette de Corbie who had kept Yolande informed about the little girl since her arrival in the Darc household. There was Gérard Manchet, the dauphin's confessor, the ex-chancellor Le Maçon, Cardinal Gerson, and Raoul de Gaucourt, the confidant of Jehanne's half-brother Charles, Duke of Orleans. Gaucourt, being permitted to visit Charles in England whenever he pleased, could keep the head of the Orleans family actively collaborating. and fully informed of all their plans.

France had not lacked successful woman warriors. Who had not heard of Jehanne de Monfort, a twenty-three-year-old whose husband was taken prisoner in 1341 when defending Hennebout against Charles de Blois? She personally took over the defence and charged out of the castle at the head of her cavalry, trounced her opponents by a clever manoeuvre, and obliged them to raise the siege. Then she made the assembled Breton noblemen acknowledge that her three-year-old son was the legitimate Duke of Brittany! Then again, in 1345 Jehanne de Belleville, learning that her husband had been beheaded by King Philippe VI, raised an army at Nantes, took six castles by storm and killed their garrisons to the last man. She then equipped a ship and became a privateer, attacking and sinking every French ship she encountered. There were many other women one could recall who had become successful fighters.

For Yolande to produce at the right moment a romantic young Princess of Orleans who would lead troops to victory was, therefore, a reasonable enough proposition seeing what promising material Jehanne looked to provide.

47

But further thought revealed fatal flaws in this plan. Wouldn't people want to know why as a healthy baby she had been spirited away from Paris to Domremy and secretly brought up there? Wouldn't it militate against her popular support that Isabeau, hated and despised by so many people with such good reason, was her mother? Yolande and her friends knew that she was a full sister of the dauphin, but did they want to run the risk of Jehanne's adulterine status stimulating further controversy over Charles's legitimacy? After all, there was only a four year gap between their ages. Surely, the less that subject was raked over the better.

Might not Jehanne have an equal or even greater popular appeal if she were the artless daughter of common people? The child, say, of some poor labourer, untutored, listening to the tales of travellers stopping to rest in Domremy, talking of poor people like herself suffering because of the war? . . . Or better still perhaps, listening to the Mendicant Friars – she would be pious, wouldn't she? . . . Then why not directly inspired by Heaven? . . . Ah, why not indeed? . . . Wouldn't a shepherdess be still more appropriate? For then she could hear heavenly voices while watching over her father's sheep. . . . Yes . . . To invoke the miraculous would be a very real, indeed, a tremendous advantage . . . Furthermore, a leader sent by God would be neutral as far as the various princes were concerned, and few would object to serving under a divine choice.

Probably it was Colette who pointed out that this plan too contained a devastating flaw. It ignored the fact that Jehanne had been encouraged to develop attitudes consonant with being a nun. She was deeply religious. It was quite unthinkable to suppose that she would be willing to claim divine inspiration when really it was no more than make believe, indeed, a deliberate plan designed to mislead and deceive simple people whose help and possible sacrifice were being invoked. She would regard it as blasphemy. Even if she agreed it was for a good cause, it would still conflict with her youthful idealism. Simply to tell Jehanne of the part she was to play and expect her cooperation was out of the question. I am sure Yolande would have agreed with this and then added, 'Well then, we must convince the child that she IS divinely inspired . . . Don't you think, Colette if you . . .'

48

During the summer after Jehanne's thirteenth birthday she was competing one morning with other village children, running races in a field by the river. A little boy she did not remember having seen before told her that her mother wanted her to come at once – so she ran back to the castle only to be told that Isabelle had sent no such message, and she could return forthwith to the races. As she was walking back through the garden, wondering why she should have been tricked in this way, she heard her name being called 'Jehanne! Jehanne!' It was a most unusual voice, very distinct and entrancingly beautiful. Jehanne stopped, wondering where the voice was coming from, it seemed to be from the direction of the church. And then she noticed a kind of radiance, in the same direction, as though there were a bright light behind and to the right side of her.

She described later how the Voice which claimed to be a voice from Heaven, continued to address her and repeated its message three times. But its import was extremely vague according to the replies she first gave at the trial in Rouen. It is, however, possible to deduce from Jehanne's behaviour and later statements, that she was told she must keep herself pure and guard her behaviour because she had been chosen by the Lord of Heaven for a very special task. She would have to go to France to help the dauphin. She must go often to the chapel at Bermont, and she must tell no one – not even her parents or her confessor, that she had heard this Voice.

It has to be remembered that the fifteenth century was probably the most superstitious period in European history. Saints and devils were almost commonplace, anyone might meet them; witchcraft was a frightening reality. The teaching of the Church was taken literally. Visionaries who related their experiences were listened to with respect, prophesies were believed quite seriously. Miracles and apparitions, sorcery and love-potions were fundamental tenets underlying much popular thought.

As she listened to the Voice, Jehanne said she became terrified, and she found the experience all the more unnerving because it was midday and the sun was shining. Why, one wonders, did she feel so frightened? Perhaps she remembered that strange little boy who had tricked her, and asked herself if this was part of the same thing? Yet that Voice hadn't sounded in the least as though it was making fun of her. And that light, that radiance in the same place as the voice. Could it really have been a message from Heaven? Had she, Jehanne, really been singled out by the Lord of Heaven? She dared not believe it. Might it not more likely be some dreadful kind of temptation devised by Satan to destroy her? How often had she secretly wished that she had been born a boy, free to go out into the world and have exciting adventures like many of those she had heard tell. And if the message were really from Heaven, why should she be forbidden to tell her parents or confessor? That really did seem like something she must remember and beware of. Hadn't she been warned that temptations were often dressed up like something wonderful and good? Should she go to St Marie of Bermont? If she went there and was asked why she had gone, what would she say? Wouldn't she have to tell a lie or refuse to answer? Might a demon be waiting for her there? She did not dare to go.

Three days later the experience was repeated, though I do not know where. It added to her wild alarm. Then this was followed a few days later by a much more memorable and astonishing experience. St Michael himself in shining armour, accompanied by angels and saints wearing exquisite crowns visited her, and at last she was convinced that her Voice was the voice of an angel, and it really did come from Heaven. Saint Michael promised her that Saint Catherine and Saint Margaret would come to help her in future. After this I am sure she hurried to the Hermitage of Bermont, and there was dear Mère Colette. She did not ask her why she had come, but said she was glad to see her because the time had arrived when she was old enough to be told who her real mother was and who her father had been.

I feel sure that the voice Jehanne heard in the garden was that of Colette making use of her angelic *ton céleste*.[5] But Colette had nothing to do with the radiance Jehanne was aware of while she listened to that voice. That radiance can explain Jehanne's subsequent Voices and the extraordinary steadfastness she exhibited in maintaining her stance and the unremitting cooperation she showed in playing her part in Yolande's plans.

In a cattle raising district like the Barrois, bovine tuberculosis would have been an endemic disease. Jehanne like many other children growing up there might well have become infected and as a result developed tubercular abscesses. Being a robust and well-fed child her body could have reacted in the way many young victims' do, by encysting the lesions with a hard cheesy substance which forms an impermeable barrier to the toxins produced and prevents further spread of the bacteria. In this way she would have been 'cured'.

Such cysts are called tuberculomas. They are usually formed in people under twenty years of age. Normally the cysts remain unnoticed but should one be located inside the skull near the left temple, typical indications of its presence may occur. It so happens that the nerves conveying messages from the sense organs of sight, hearing, taste, touch and smell lie extremely close to one another there, so that disease in that area – a tumour, a tuberculoma, a blood clot in a small artery or scar tissue say – may cause spurious messages to give rise to hallucinations.[6] Patients with untreated tumours or active abscesses soon exhibit graver symptoms and seldom survive very long, but a tuberculoma once formed can remain harmless and change very little over the years. The sensation of a light coming from one side is a frequently observed symptom of people with a tuberculoma there.

It has also been found that nerves in this 'sensitized' condition may be stimulated by flickering light, so it is not unreasonable to suppose that bright sunlight twinkling through leafy treetops may enhance the probability of a hallucination occurring or make it more intense. Jehanne mentioned that sometimes she did not understand what her Voices were saying until she went into the woods. At first she experienced her contact with her Voices two or three times a week, but during her trial in Rouen they occurred several times a day. Hallucinations due to tuberculomas tend to become more frequent as time passes. There is good reason to suppose then, that Jehanne had a tuberculoma in that critical area. That her hallucinations became manifest just at the time of her 'revelation' in the garden, was Yolande's providential good fortune.

When Jehanne for the second time heard the Voice repeating the message it was even more alarming. It is not to be supposed that Colette was responsible for it on that

51

occasion. But remembering the state of anxiety Jehanne was in after her first experience, it is only to be expected that if she had had an auditory hallucination a few days later, it would have been profoundly influenced by what had happened before. But the second hallucination – that is, her third 'supernatural' experience – relieved her anxieties completely.[7] She would have regarded this as an answer to her desperate prayers for help, and it is a measure of her great faith that help would surely be vouchsafed. (We might also regard it as a clear example of wish fulfilment!)

When real people gave her advice, or even told her things, I believe she discussed it with her Voices, and maybe asked their opinion as to whether she should take it or believe what was said or no. This could well have encouraged her mental development a great deal and enabled her later to take quick and risky decisions without hesitation. It would also explain why she was apt to attribute to her Voices information that must clearly have been given initially by real people with whom she had been in contact. I believe too, that much of the time she apparently spent in prayer in numerous churches, was devoted to communicating with her Voices, or at least trying to get into contact with them.

What is abundantly clear is that Jehanne herself was absolutely certain that she was privileged to be in contact with the Lord of Heaven, sometimes through the presence of Saint Margaret and Saint Catherine, often through a Voice and very occasionally, with the archangel Saint Michael himself. The choice of saint is doubtless to be attributed to her familiarity with St Margaret in the church at Domremy, and St Catherine in the larger church at Greux. And Saint Michael himself was, after all, the patron saint of France.

Not that her new life style after Saint Michael visited her was free from anxieties. There were quite new ones instead. Of course she no longer had time to play with the other children, but that didn't matter. And there were compensations. Clearly she had been provided with the best possible way of undoing the harm that her mother had done to France. And if she did succeed in helping the dauphin it would show that she was certainly fit to be a member of the great House of Orleans. What was really alarming was the fact that she had suddenly found herself burdened with an immense responsibility from which she couldn't escape. She had had to promise to be an unbelievably well-behaved and good girl, and not get married until such time as she had dealt with all the dauphin's problems that God wanted her to settle, admittedly with God's help. Of course it was marvellous to have St Catherine and St Margaret like that, but if she wasn't good all the time would they still come to her? She didn't know, and they didn't know either.

But when it was all finished she would be free to marry and have a family. That was far better than being a Poor Clare. But when would that be? Her Saints thought that she would be quite grown up, but they didn't know when. She wouldn't be able to live with herself if she failed and they stopped coming. But surely if God told her he wanted her to do something it wouldn't be impossible to do it. As for her promise to be good, if she went to confession whenever she had the chance, it would mean she was not going far wrong, wouldn't it? Of course people would laugh at her for being too pious, but need that bother her? If they really knew why she was doing it they wouldn't laugh, would they?

Later when it became clear that she would certainly be involved with actual fighting I believe that she was assured THAT SHE WOULD NOT GET KILLED, though she might get wounded, but not all that badly. After all, if she was dead she wouldn't be able to do what God wanted, would she? It made sense.

She had had no idea how many cousins and aunts and stepsisters and brothers she had got. And they were really HERS. One of the delightful things in the future would be getting to know them. Meanwhile, all these exciting things had to be kept secret, so her behaviour mustn't change in spite of them. She must still call Isabelle and Jacques mother and father as though they were, and do what they wanted. But one of these days . . . Goody!

5

Preparation

Colette was mainly responsible for Jehanne's changed education. She was coached by Jean Collin, the scholarly vicar of Greux – the village on the other bank of the Meuse in Lorraine – until he was promoted to be dean of the seminary college in Dieulouard. The chatelains in the district co-operated with Colette in supervising Jehanne's lessons in deportment when Colette was away, teaching her the proper obeisances to make and to whom, the correct modes of address and rules of precedence, and probably the medieval peculiarities equivalent to our upper class conventions. She was welcomed as a visitor in the great houses in the neighbourhood, amongst others by Agnes de Joinville who was married to Claude d'Essay, and Jehanne de Bauffremont, wife of André de Joinville, and Alarde de Chambley, wife of Robert de Baudricourt, commandant of the castle at Vaucouleurs. It is likely that Jehanne, then eighteen, was invited to their wedding in Vaucouleurs, and one wonders if on that, and perhaps other occasions, she met Robert des Armoises the bride's handsome twenty-year-old cousin, and found him attractive, perhaps even her *beau idéal*.

But I believe the most exciting and enjoyable activity that was introduced into her new way of life was learning to ride and manage horses. She inherited her father's prowess. She emulated and equalled his spectacular leap into the saddle, scorning the use of a stirrup. She became able immediately to establish rapport with any horse as soon as she mounted it. Her teacher was an equerry who was a member of Yolande's entourage, called Bertrand de Poulengy. He lived in the neighbourhood and was a friend of Baudricourt and was officially attached to his garrison. Incidentally he had probably acted as an unostentatious security guard while Jehanne was a young child. Later another equerry called variously Jean de Metz or Novelonpont, joined them and trained her in the use of weapons and the lance in jousting, and they all had discussions on military strategy and tactics, particularly the management of those newfangled weapons called cannon, which employed gunpowder and which could actually breach stone walls. Jehanne found this absorbingly interesting.

In 1427 when she was twenty, Jehanne was sued for breach of promise by a young man who had made many unsuccessful proposals of marriage to her. Some people said Jacques Darc would have been pleased had she married him. She defended herself in court and won, having gone alone to Toul where the case was heard. She rode there and back the same day on horseback, a distance of some eighty kilometres. It is worth noting that had she been a minor at this time, she could not have defended herself, but would have needed an adult to undertake her defence.

Jehanne always rode astride. She was more fortunate than most women riders in that she escaped those ills to which their flesh is normally heir. She never menstruated.[8] I think it very probable that she discussed this with her saints and linked it with her solemnly made vow of virginity which she had made to the King of Heaven and which she would keep until He allowed her to rescind it. When this time came, I believe she was convinced that she would then be subject to a miracle and become as other women were.

All this time she was experiencing her hallucinations, certain that they were designed to help her play her part in the liberation of the French people and her family. That the Lord of Heaven was guiding her friends – though she doubted if they were aware of it in the way she was – was clear when she found her dear Mère Colette in the little chapel at Bermont. When she learned things first from her 'real' teachers, St Margaret and St Catherine normally confirmed what she had been told. Sometimes I believe the saints informed her of something first. Didn't St Margaret remind her that she herself had worn men's clothing in Antioch and advise Jehanne, when she began campaigning, to do the same – an idea Jehanne adopted with enthusiasm? I doubt if she thought it necessary to report this to her friends as it would be difficult, if it were not approved of, to argue convincingly without mentioning her revelations. Its practicality was obvious and when the time came it was actually accepted by all the people about her without demur.

As time passed she was initiated into all sorts of personal and state secrets. She was told of the treaty with Scotland and that Scottish troops were coming to France to help the dauphin, and of the proposed marriage with the Scottish princess. Increasingly she felt herself to be part of the great family that constituted the House of Orleans. She longed to bring about the release of her half-brother. Her saints told her a great deal about him, and she was told that she would be permitted to tell him about her revelations, just as she would be able to tell the dauphin Charles, whom she now knew was her brother. She wondered if they would be able to see her saints and hear their voices as she did. She had observed that occasionally, when she was with other people, the saints came and went amongst them, but no one else seemed to be aware of them in the way she was. Occasionally the saints were just like other people, real people, and on one such occasion she had asked St Catherine to touch the ring Mère Colette had given her, and she had actually touched it; it was engraved with the names Jhesus-Maria and three crosses. This immeasurably increased its value in the eyes of its owner. Jehanne also came into possession of another ring at some time, engraved with the Orleans arms, and it is suggested by some that her father was wearing it when he was assassinated.

Jehanne's religious education was not neglected in this period. When she was fourteen she was accepted as a novitiate into the Third Order, and by the time she was ready to leave Domremy had graduated into the class of *Dame Très Discrète*. It was agreed that when she was ready to lead France to victory she would carry the standard of the Third Order of St Francis, so that not only would she have soldiers behind her but also the multitude of people in cities and the countryside who belonged to the Third Order. She had learned the use of signs and passwords which enabled members to recognize each other, know whom they could trust, and what words they should use in a special way to convey a secret meaning understood only by the initiated.

While Jehanne was growing up Yolande was marshalling formidable forces to support her when she should appear in public, making use of her far-flung network of informants and emissaries – the Mendicant Friars and members of the Third Order. Widespread changes in attitude caused by decades of destructive war and the Black Death had taken place in France. When the Hundred Years War had begun there was no difference between English and French barons. They both spoke French and they all accepted the same feudal rights and obligations. But by the 1420s this no longer held. The English spoke English and the French, French. The English had plundered the countryside, decimated the French nobility and ruined many families by exorbitant ransoms and pillage. Hatred of the English invader was widespread and growing. But the English rulers had introduced in the towns under their control, progressive reforms and enlightened changes which had won the support of institutions like the University of Paris, organizations of merchants and members of the legal profession, traders and craftsmen's guilds.

When France had been composed of prosperous provinces the ordinary people had relied upon their overlords to protect them, but war and pestilence had so impoverished the aristocracy this was often no longer possible, so that they were obliged to provide for their own security. Necessity had led to cooperation between districts, accompanied by an awareness of their all being French. The idea of nationality had come into being.

Again because of war and pestilence, large areas of France had been denuded of priests, and the inhabitants found themselves bereft of necessary sacred rights and ceremonies. Mendicant Friars had been foremost in providing help and guidance in such districts and had built up a special relationship with ordinary folk as a result. So they were well placed to disseminate fresh ideas, news and rumours throughout the countryside.

Stories about King Arthur and his knights were widely known, and his counsellor, Merlin, was a highly esteemed prophet. When it got about that a prophecy of his had been

57

discovered in a book saying, 'France would be lost by a woman and saved by a woman', Isabeau easily slipped into the first part of this prediction and someone to carry out the second part was awaited with eager confidence. A virgin from the borders of Lorraine was then mentioned, and this was later narrowed to a virgin associated with a *Bois Chenu* – referring to an ancient tree in the woods near Domremy where the ladies of the Third Order sometimes gathered, and where their children used to take part on some special Sunday in the summer in a traditional ceremony of decorating the tree with flowers, dancing around it and singing songs.

Then the virgin became a shepherdess who heard heavenly voices as she sat in the fields on the borders of Lorraine while watching her father's sheep. When later the Voices told her to go to France to help the French king and relieve Orleans, everyone knew for certain that she was the virgin foretold by Merlin. Anticipation and excitement seized people hitherto lacking all hope and initiative.

The role foretold for Jehanne was not only spread by word of mouth. In a consul's register for 1428/29 in the city of Albi there is a document which has the appearance of coming from the Chancellery. 'In the month of March 1429 there presented herself to the noble king of France a young maid aged some fourteen or fifteen years – who was from the country and duchy of Lorraine, which country is situated on the frontier of Germany. And the said maid was an ignorant shepherdess who had spent all her time guarding sheep.'

It is recorded that Yolande made many journeys to Lorraine during the later years when Jehanne was living in Domremy. I think we may safely assume that she and Jehanne became intimately acquainted then. One can imagine the impact this beautiful and forceful personality had on Jehanne, who always spoke of her as 'my queen' and for whom her loyalty never wavered.

Yolande would have encouraged Jehanne's identification with the House of Orleans and stressed the responsibilities of blue blood. She probably explained that although Charles was her full brother, because Roman law maintained that *'is pater est quem nuptiae demonstrant'* – whoever is born in wedlock can prove who is his father – the Treaty of Troyes was wrong to disinherit him. But because not everyone knew or understood

Roman law, and because of the strong position that the English had established (and it had to be remembered that English law was different from French law anyway), it was very important that the fact that the late duke of Orleans was really his father and hers, should not be known. It would only help the English. This was why it was essential that Jehanne should never reveal who her real parents were.

I believe that Yolande would also have emphasized how imperative it was that Charles should be crowned in Rheims Cathedral. If he were crowned there and anointed with the Holy Oil that had been miraculously sent from Heaven for Clovis's baptism, no one would doubt that it was Charles whom the King of Heaven wanted to have on the French throne, for since Clovis's time every French king had been anointed with it. Charles himself did not seem to understand how important this was, so Jehanne must always address him as dauphin, just to emphasize it.

Doubtless Yolande also confirmed that according to the Mendicant Friars people all over the country were eagerly talking about Merlin's prophecy, identifying the evil woman with Isabeau and the saviour with a virgin from Lorraine. Hermine of Rheims had said that the virgin from Lorraine would come soon to help the king of France to get back his kingdom. And others had foretold that the virgin was a shepherdess who heard heavenly voices to guide her. Jehanne would agree, would she not, that metaphorically speaking she could be called a shepherdess, carrying out the will of Heaven to help the people? Indeed might she not say that voices from Heaven guided and inspired her? Yes, Jehanne could in all sincerity agree, she could indeed.

Did Yolande know that St Catherine and St Margaret regularly visited Jehanne? Or did she suppose the voice Jehanne had heard in the garden years ago was the sole source of her belief in her destiny and her steadfastness? I do not know, but I think it unlikely that Jehanne had told her.

I think there is evidence that Yolande also told Jehanne that she could rely upon receiving military help for some months only, which should be long enough to get to Rheims and crown Charles. But she must not forget that the time was limited for the simple reason that by that time their funds would have run out. But after the coronation Jehanne would be free to live her own life as she saw fit.

6

The Campaign Begins

I think there is evidence that at times Jehanne's saints did not agree with her human advisors. For instance, she believed the time had come to go to Chinon in 1428 when she had tried and failed to persuade Robert de Baudricourt to provide her with an escort. She even got permission to tell him that she had revelations from God telling her to go. She still failed to convince him.

Jacques Darc was troubled by nightmares that she was attempting to go to Chinon with a lot of soldiers and seriously threatened to have her drowned by her brothers rather than allow it – one of the reasons why I think it unlikely that he knew her real parentage.

The following year a niece of Isabelle Romée called Aveline de Vouton was soon to have a baby. She welcomed Jehanne's offer to come and make herself useful, and Jacques made no objection. While there, Jehanne persuaded the father to be, Durant Laxart, to accompany her to Vaucouleurs to see Robert de Baudricourt again. It was only a league from Burey-le-Petit. Robert knew that he had to wait until he had a signal from Yolande and it had not come. Perhaps because he felt it safest to avoid any dangerous rumours circulating he pretended to complete ignorance, and once more she had to return to Domremy.

But some months later she was again advised by her saints that she should go to Chinon, and this time, according to the evidence she gave in Rouen, they left it to her to decide whether or not she should tell her parents that she was going to Vaucouleurs again. She decided to leave unannounced, which caused them great alarm, and she minimized this as best she could by writing them a long letter, whereupon she was forgiven. By this time speculations about a virgin were rife and Robert evidently thought it was safe to cooperate, so he arranged and paid for her to lodge with some simple people called Catherine and Henri le Royer. He probably explained that it was not advisable for a simple shepherdess to stay in the castle as a guest of his wife and himself. Meanwhile a lively correspondence took place between Baudricourt, his good friend René d'Anjou, who at that time was living at Pont-à-Mousson, and Charles II Duke of Lorraine. We know from archives that Robert paid a courier five sols six deniers for bringing him a letter on January 29th 1429 containing a safe-conduct for Jehanne to visit the Duke at Nancy.

Jean Novelonpont de Metz was detailed to accompany her for the first part of her journey. They set out on February 1st and stayed that night in a hostelry in Toul, the Fleur-du-Lys. There they met Jean de Dieulouard, an equerry sent by René d'Anjou, who accompanied her for the rest of the way to Nancy.

They arrived at Dieulouard that evening. She was taken to the College of Saint Laurent in the Place des Moines where she was magnificently entertained by the Dean, Jean Collin, who had earlier coached her when he was the vicar of Greux. He had been the brother-in-law of her foster sister Catherine Darc, who had died the previous year. He insisted on emptying his purse into Jehanne's when she left 'to help her on her journey.' Jean de Dieulouard spent the night in his family home, also in the Place des Moines.

When they arrived in Nancy she was treated as a princess, and immediately taken to the duke. She found René d'Anjou there before her, and the three of them were soon closeted together and I believe it was then Jehanne learned what I believe was behind this unexpected invitation.

Probably before they would tell her anything, she had to understand that what she was about to hear was never to be revealed to anyone except her brother, the king. I expect they assured her that she would shortly be returning to Vaucouleurs and Yolande would soon send a messenger from Chinon, and then, Baudricourt would arrange an escort for her.

I believe she was told that when they arrived in Sainte-

Catherine-de-Fierbois, which would be their last stop before reaching Chinon, she should write a letter to the king, saying that they were about to arrive, and asking that he would receive them. She had to remember that there were any number of visionaries who offered their services to the king and requested an audience with him, but these people were always ignored and she also had to remember that he did not know that she was his sister, and this letter must not mention it. She should sign it Jehanne la Pucelle, for by now he almost certainly believed they were related, as he had received a letter from Cardinal Gerson telling him that Cardinal de Foix was shortly returning from Rome, and that Charles should try to arrange an interview with him because he had some very interesting information about the *Puella Aurelianensis* – the Maid of Orleans. (Incidentally this is the first time Orleans has been used in connection with Jehanne, and it must have been understood as a surname, for up to that time she had had no connection with the city).

And then I believe they added that while she was at Sainte-Catherine-de-Fierbois she should make a point of finding whereabouts in the church was the tomb of the knight Cligny de Bréhan, as he had been buried there with a sword engraved with five crosses. This had been a gift from the Constable du Guesclin to Jehanne's father Louis, who had bequeathed it to Bréhan. When she got to Chinon she should ask for it to be sent to her.

Yolande had arranged for her to stay at the residence of the Lady de Cougny, the widow of an important magistrate. Yolande would also arrange for Jehanne to be taken secretly to the chateau to see her and her daughter Queen Marie. There they would discuss her introduction to the Court.

Then when Jehanne was able to talk to the king privately, she must tell him that they were full brother and sister, their mother was Isabeau and their father the late Louis, Duke of Orleans. It was important that people should not know that she was his sister – she must remember they believed that she was a peasant inspired by God.

Charles was unnecessarily worried because he was not the son of Charles VI. Legally he was the rightful heir to the throne because he was born in wedlock. But more important than this was the fact that he was married to Marie of Anjou.

This made him the legitimate King of France in a much more important sense.

I think that at this point Jehanne was reminded of the promise that she had made. *What she was about to learn was quite the most potentially dangerous matter that she had got to impart to Charles.* This was a secret between them that must be kept at all costs. It was the real reason she had been brought to Lorraine. She was then assured that her informants wholeheartedly believed in the truth of what they were about to tell her, but it was regarded by the Roman Catholic Church as a heresy of the deepest die.

In spite of what the Church taught, the truth was that Jesus was a married man. In his time it was as important for wives to be found for sons, as husbands for daughters, and boys were married when they were quite young. That Jesus was not celibate was proven because he was a rabbi, a teacher, and an unmarried man could not become a rabbi. He was married to Mary Magdalene, a descendant of Benjamin, whose family had provided the earliest Jewish kings. He and Mary had had children.

Had the Romans not conquered Palestine, Jesus would have been king, for not only was he of the line of David and Solomon, but he was regarded as a prophet and messiah too. It is important to remember that the Greek word for messiah is christ, meaning a leader. It has no divine connotation.[9] The invaders had installed a puppet king, Herod, on the throne. But Jesus had a great popular following as well as much support from his peers. When he spoke of his beloved disciple he was referring to his wife. One Passover he staged a revolt which was successful for a while and he was anointed King. But his reign was short-lived and he was soon overcome. Like all captured rebels he was condemned to be crucified. But because he had been anointed, Pilate rightly addressed him as King of the Jews.

Pontius Pilate was not at all like the person portrayed in the New Testament, but a corrupt governor easy to bribe. Joseph of Arimathea paid him to allow Jesus to be crucified in his private garden, near a newly built sepulchre, and also bribed him to have permission to bury Jesus when he was dead instead of leaving him for days on the cross. When Jesus asked for a drink and was given a sponge supposedly wetted with vinegar, it contained a powerful drug which quickly made him unconscious so that the centurion thought he was dead, and allowed Joseph to take him down from the cross, though he did stab him with his spear. He was then wrapped in a shroud and put in the sepulchre, where later his friends came to take him away, and before long he recovered. It was widely believed that he would never die, but like Elijah would come again from Heaven when the world was ready to receive him.

Joseph of Arimathea and Mary Magdalene's brother Lazarus smuggled her and the children aboard a ship, and they all set sail for Marseilles which was near a long established and flourishing Jewish community, who welcomed them all and treated them as royalty. The refugees carried on the teaching of Jesus and a great many people embraced it, regarding themselves as Christians. They honoured Jesus as a great teacher and prophet, but not as divine. For Jews such a suggestion would have been blasphemous. Mary Magdalene was regarded very highly and many Christian cathedrals and churches which were dedicated to Our Lady – *Notre Dame* – were dedicated to her, not to the mother of Jesus. The same was true of the Black Virgins, then to be found in places like Puy and Liesse and Bermont.[10]

The children of Jesus and Mary married and had children and grandchildren. They did not cut their hair and many of them had remarkable powers of healing. During the fifth century one married the Frankish king who was ruling France and they gave rise to the Merovingian dynasty of French kings. They were known as the long-haired kings, and were really priest-kings, who ruled but did not govern. The government of the country was carried on by a hereditary family known as the Mayors of the Palace. The special quality of Jesus's blood was transmitted by both daughters and sons.

At this time there were a great many different kinds of Christians, and particularly in the Languedoc and in the Pyrenees there were many called Cathars who did not believe that Jesus was divine. Nor did they believe that the Cross had any special significance. They thought too that people should try to get into contact with God themselves, and not rely on faith, simply believing what the church taught them they ought to believe. Because the Muslims and Jews also believed that Jesus was a man and not divine, there was no difficulty in all three groups cooperating and tolerating each other, and they learned a great deal from each other to the great benefit of everyone. The area became a seat of learning, and most people were literate there at a time when in the rest of Europe most people could not even write their own name. The Cathars thought it was wrong to fight people or to be cruel to animals and that God believed that men and women were equally important.

The most famous Merovingian king was Clovis, and he married a Roman Catholic wife, who persuaded him to be baptized into the Roman Catholic Church. In return the pope promised that the papacy would always maintain that the rightful king of France should be a Merovingian and that there should be a single Christian kingdom throughout Europe. Thus the Holy Roman Empire was established and Clovis was the first Emperor and head of state. Because of Clovis's cooperation the influence of the Roman Catholic Church increased enormously. The papacy maintained its promise to the Merovingians for two hundred and fifty years, but when a king called Dagobert II was on the throne, the then Mayor of the Palace, called Pepin the Fat, arranged for his murder, and the papacy reneged on its promise and recognized Pepin's son as king. The Carolingian dynasty was established as a result. Because they were aware that they were usurpers, Pepin III and Charlemagne both took care ostentatiously to marry Merovingian princesses.

But the direct Merovingian line had not been exterminated, as Dagobert's son Sigisbert by his second wife, unknown to Pepin, survived and had descendants. When the corruption and arrogance of the Roman Catholic Church had led to a great increase in the number of people in France and Germany becoming Cathars, the pope Innocent III organized the Albigensian Crusade and for eleven dreadful years thousands of people, men, women and children, were indiscriminately massacred. The countryside became virtually depopulated, and the admirable civilization that had been built up was destroyed and the cruel Inquisition came into being. Since that time it had become a dangerous heresy to believe that Jesus had been a man.

One of Sigisbert's direct descendants was Godfroi de Bouillon, a leader of the First Crusade which conquered Jerusalem and the surrounding countryside. When the new state of Jerusalem was established there, he was asked to be king, but though he became its ruler, he refused the title. In a way one could say that he was claiming his heritage for he was a direct descendant of Jesus who had been the last rightful king of Jerusalem. Godfroi had sold up all his lands and possessions in France before he left for the Crusade, which suggests he had had every intention of settling there.

Anyway, the state of Jerusalem under Godfroi de Bouillon was organized on the original Christian lines, with a ruler having limited powers, the ordinary people having control over their fiscal affairs, and the poor and vulnerable were cherished and looked after, and this included animals. In fact, an effort was made to bring about the Kingdom of Heaven upon Earth.

One can imagine how intently Jehanne listened to these revelations, and how easily she could have identified her own experiences with the Cathar belief that it was better to have direct access to God than to base one's beliefs on what the church taught. To hear that Jesus was not divine, when clearly He was actually in Heaven, would seem to her rather like splitting hairs, and I doubt if it had any disturbing effect on her. She was very conscious of the relief she had felt when she was saved from having to become a nun and may well have felt pleased, perhaps not consciously realizing why, when she heard that Jesus and Mary had had a family.

When Godfroi died and his brother Baudouin became the ruler, he did take the title King of Jerusalem, and the heads of the European countries acknowledged it had an equal precedence with their own. Though Jerusalem fell to the Saracens quite a long time ago, the title still persisted for Baudouin's direct descendants, and René d'Anjou now held it, just as Yolande enjoyed the title Queen of Jerusalem, because her husband had been King of Jerusalem when he was alive.

René was also the Grand Master of a secret society called the Priory of Sion.[11] It was known to very few people. It was founded by Godfroi de Bouillon in Jerusalem with the aim of restoring the Merovingian dynasty in France so that the country could be governed in the same way as the State of Jerusalem had been. Also the church would be reorganized so that corrupt and wealthy bishops and cardinals would be removed, and they would not be allowed to hold hundreds of benefices at the expense of the poor clergy. It was believed that when the Kingdom of Heaven was established on Earth, that Jesus would come back again to rule it.

Soon after Godfroi was installed in Jerusalem he also founded the Order of the Templars. Originally they were the bodyguard of the people who had the sacred blood of Jesus in their veins. They lived in part of the Temple in Jerusalem, and probably discovered secrets buried there. Later the Templars became the military arm of the Priory of Sion, intending to establish the Kingdom of Heaven on Earth, and to this end the organization became rich and powerful, which excited the greed and fear of Philippe IV king of France because he owed them a lot of money. As the only person who had the right to disband the Templars was the Pope, and he did not want to do it, Philippe had him murdered, and the same fate befell his successor for the same reason. But Philippe next time managed to get his own nominee elected as pope Clement V, and then the Order was disbanded. Philippe did his best to have all the Templars killed, and to a great extent he succeeded, but he did not manage to get his hands on their wealth, most of which disappeared along with nearly all their documents. Not a few of the Templars found refuge in the Franciscan Order, and their ideals and insignia were adopted by them and the Third Order. The square cross in a circle was a Merovingian emblem and was adopted by the Templars, and now it was a sign of the Third Order and the Franciscans.

'This is all quite enthralling, but why should this cure Charles's distress over his undoubted illegitimacy?' Jehanne would have asked.

'Because when you have carried out the commandment of the Lord of Heaven to have him crowned in RHEIMS, where all the French kings have been crowned and anointed with the Holy Oil used in Clovis's baptism since the time of Charlemagne's father, it will be impossible for the Church or anyone else to say that he is not the king whom God wishes to have on the French throne. And Charles's heir, HIS child, will have Merovingian blood in his veins. He will be a direct descendant of Jesus. He will be the first rightful French king since Dagobert II.'

The following day the Lorraine Court was invited to witness a display of Jehanne's horsemanship. I wish I knew how she was introduced. She astounded everyone by her skill and daring, and naturally displayed her unique capacity for leaping into the saddle. Then she was challenged to a joust and her skill with the lance astonished her audience. At the end of her demonstration the Duke presented her with a magnificent black horse. It was a destrier, a breed reserved exclusively for the use of royalty and the noblest aristocracy. The Duke also gave her four gold francs. It is said she asked for René d'Anjou to escort her to Chinon, but this was not granted, though it is to be remembered that he did take part in the relief of Orleans.

A few days later she and Dieulouard, with his valet Julien, returned to Vaucouleurs, Jehanne riding her fabulous new mount. She visited a Black Virgin shrine on their journey back to Vaucouleurs where they arrived on February 13th. Her escort remained there with her.

Impatient to be off she went again to Robert de Baudricourt and begged him to send her to Chinon, insisting that the dauphin had suffered a terrible reverse. In fact it was true – the English the day before had been delivering a quantity of food supplies suitable for use during Lent to the troops besieging Orleans. At the end of a hard day's fighting the French had to acknowledge a resounding defeat, known to history as the Battle of the Herrings. Whether Jehanne's information was due to second sight or pigeon post is anyone's guess. She was credited with clairvoyance at times, but I find myself unconvinced. Her pleas for an escort on this occasion were as usual ignored.

But about that time a royal messenger called Collet de Vienne left Chinon for Vaucouleurs, and on that same day the Bastard of Orleans, now responsible for the defence of the city since Clermont's disgrace over the Battle of the Herrings, also left Chinon for Orleans. On his arrival there he roused the enthusiasm of the inhabitants by telling them that a virgin was shortly coming from Lorraine to lift their siege. On February 19th Collet de Vienne arrived in Vaucouleurs – and Baudricourt immediately produced his plans. Jean Novelonpont de Metz was in charge of the expedition, and he was accompanied by Bertrand de Poulengy, Jean de Dieulouard, Collet de Vienne, Pierre Darc, a Scottish archer called Richard, and Dieulouard's valet Julien. Jehanne had had her hair cut short like a page, and was dressed in male clothing that had been made for her. Robert presented her with a sword. They set out on the evening of February 23rd. It was necessary for them to do most of their travelling by night because they were traversing territory controlled by the Burgundians or the English. They spent most of their days in Franciscan monasteries. The first one they visited was in charge of an uncle of Baudricourt. It is said that Colette de Corbie had already made the arrangements for their journey.

It took them eleven days to travel the 150 leagues. They went via Clairvaux, Tonnerre, Auxerre, Gien, Loches and arrived at Sainte-Catherine-de-Fierbois on Friday March 4th. Jehanne spent part of the night writing a letter to the king, which was delivered the following morning, probably by Collet de Vienne. Jehanne went to mass three times that day, and spent much of her time praying in the church (or so it is recorded). Subsequent events lead one to suppose that during this time she located the tomb of Cligny de Bréhan behind the altar.

They arrived in Chinon about midday on March 6th, and Jehanne, Novelonpont, and Poulengy sat down to a meal in the de Cougny household. Afterwards the men visited their friend the chief equerry, Gobert Thiébaut, who later took them to the king's confessor, Gérard Machet, one of Yolande's staunchest allies. After talking together for some time he took them to see the king.

When they had been introduced Novelonpont produced a letter from Robert de Baudricourt which he said was for the king's eyes alone. It is said that it told the king that La Pucelle had come from Domremy in the company of these gentlemen who had paid all the expenses of the journey themselves, having been chosen to take her safely to Chinon by Baudricourt. Afterwards they had a considerable talk, their expenses were reimbursed and themselves and the rest of the party were invited to stay at Chinon at the Treasury's expense until such time as they would leave for Orleans.

Meanwhile Jehanne found herself quietly taken to the Queen's quarters in the chateau, where doubtless Yolande and Marie d'Anjou heard about her visit to Lorraine, the wonderful characteristics of her destrier, the long journey to Chinon, and the sword which had belonged to her father which she believed was to be found in a tomb behind the altar in Sainte-Catherine-de-Fierbois's church. Then she would have learned how she was to be introduced to the Court, how she must wear the simple clothes that she had travelled in, in order to produce the proper sense of shock amongst the extravagantly dressed courtiers. It was stressed that it was important for her to remember all the time to address Charles as dauphin, not king . . . Would noble dauphin perhaps be better? Yes, it might well be . . .

Then I am sure Jehanne was told that after the introductory pleasantries Charles would stroll with her into an embrasure where she could talk perfectly frankly and at ease, because Marie and Yolande had made certain that though the assembled company could see everything quite clearly – and that was essential – it would be impossible for them to hear a single word that was said. And it didn't matter in the least how long she took over this vitally important interview.

Jehanne alone stayed in the de Cougny household until she was received in Court. Novelonpont and Poulengy stayed with their friend the chief equerry. The others' lodgings are not mentioned.

At the time Jehanne came to Chinon the king's favourite was an aristocrat called Georges de la Tremouille. He came of an ancient noble family whose members had distinguished themselves since the eleventh century by their loyalty to the French kings. Georges was the younger son and had been captured at Agincourt. While he showed himself to be valiant in the field, he had not inherited any of his ancestors' admirable moral qualities. While he was imprisoned in

71

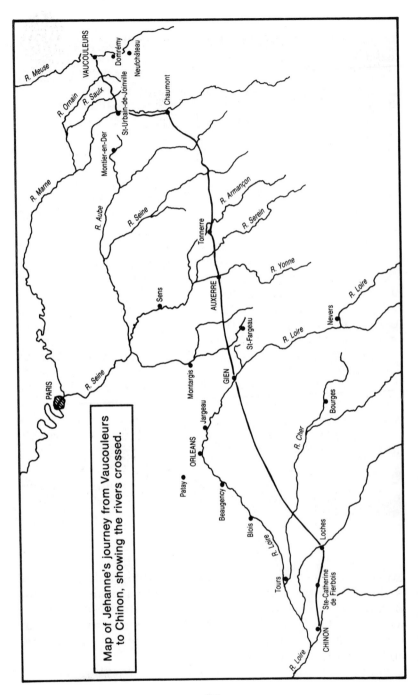

Map of Jehanne's journey from Vaucouleurs to Chinon, showing the rivers crossed.

The Castle of Chinon

London he had become friendly with his fellow captive Arthur de Richemont, the younger brother of the Duke of Brittany. La Tremouille convinced Richemont that when he was released he had the firm intention of getting in touch with Charles VI's court, his sympathies being wholly with the king and not with the Burgundians.

Quite soon after La Tremouille was ransomed he was

appointed Governor of the Dauphiné, thanks to his having become a boon companion of the then dauphin, Louis, Duke of Guyenne. La Tremouille soon became notorious for organising grossly extravagant banquets at a time when the ordinary inhabitants of Paris were in danger of dying of hunger, and he was only rescued from being put to death during the Cabochian riots by the good offices of Jean sans Peur, who had provoked the troubles. La Tremouille then decided it was time to ally himself to the Burgundians. After the murder of the dauphin however, he returned to Charles VI's Court. When Isabeau's promiscuity finally led to her being incarcerated in a convent at Monmoutier after her scandalous love affair with Louis de Boisredon in January 1417, La Tremouille, Pierre de Giac and some other young nobleman constituted her 'guards'. But in November they took part in her 'rescue', delivering her (with her glad consent) to Jean sans Peur in Troyes. When later she moved to Paris La Tremouille accompanied her there. But when Charles became the dauphin and was declared Regent, his troops managed to take possession of La Tremouille's castle in Sully (which he had been ordered by Burgundy to defend). Having then found himself Charles's prisoner, he decided it was time to change his allegiance again and he took an oath of fidelity to the Regent!

At that time Yolande was in Provence. Later La Tremouille met Pierre de Giac again and learned Giac had recently been appointed to the Regent's Council. Apparently this was by way of remuneration for the part unwittingly played by his wife, Jeanne de Naillac, when she had been Jean sans Peur's mistress, and had provided the opportunity for Jean's assassination. The pair had left the Burgundian Court after the murder.

In 1425 when Yolande returned to Bourges, La Tremouille was the king's chamberlain. Richemont recommended him, on account of his being related to both parties, to head a delegation to the Burgundian Court to propose an accord with Philippe, and offer an appropriate reparation for the death of Jean sans Peur. Burgundy would have nothing to do with this. La Tremouille fell into the hands of the English on his way back to Bourges, which caused him very considerable delay. When he did arrive he found Richemont, the Constable

74

of France, extremely unpopular with the king, and Giac had been appointed to Tremouille's post of chief chamberlain in August 1425, and was now Charles's favourite. However, Giac succeeded in behaving so outrageously – he murdered his wife in an appallingly sadistic way, and then promptly married his mistress – that La Tremouille willingly acceded to Richemont's request to get rid of him. In February 1427 he arranged a handful of men to capture Giac one night while he was in bed, and after a farcical trial he was condemned to be drowned. Because Giac had promised the Devil his right hand after his death, his executioners obligingly cut it off before sewing him up in a sack and throwing him into the river. La Tremouille married Giac's widow two months later.

Four months after this Charles bestowed his favour on an elderly man called Le Camus de Beaulieu working in his stables, whom he promoted to be Charles, Chief Equerry and Captain of Poitiers. He was soon eliminated in his turn, and he was thrown into the Clain too, after being killed with a sword and dagger, actually within sight of the king, who happened to be looking out of an upstairs window.

Yolande and Richemont came to the conclusion that Charles was so constituted that he could not live without a favourite, and they chose La Tremouille to be the next. Charles said he was willing enough, but he told them he thought they would regret their advice. He was right, it was a disastrous decision for them.

La Tremouille enlisted the help of other unscrupulous and able members of the king's council and before long he had completely undermined Richemont's position, and for more than seven years the Constable was virtually exiled to his estates in Brittany and deprived of all military influence. Corruption occurred in many quarters and La Tremouille carried on secret transactions not only with the Burgundian Court, where his elder brother was chamberlain to the duke, but even with the invaders. This came to light when the English occupied the territory around Orleans, for La Tremouille's castle of Sully was not molested in any way. And earlier, in 1427, it was remembered that a relative of his, Rochefort, had inexplicably handed over to the English, without a fight, the castle at Etampes for which he was responsible.

La Tremouille found an ally after his own heart in Regnault de Chartres. He was an unctuous, crafty individual who by flattery and malpractice had been appointed Archbishop of Rheims. But he was unable to touch the revenues of his archbishopric because it was all in Burgundian hands. So he set out to convince Charles that his only hope of saving his crown was to negotiate with the Duke of Burgundy at whatever cost. A third reliable conspirator was the Governor of Orleans, Raoul de Gaucourt.

7

Introduction to the French Court

I believe that Yolande, fully aware of Charles's unreliable character and the extent to which his disreputable favourites influenced him, had taken great pains to keep him in complete ignorance both that he had a sister and of his Bonne Mère's plans with respect to her. I think it probable that the letter mentioning the Maid of Orleans was part of Yolande's conspiracy, with the aim of suggesting to him that there might be yet another illegitimate offspring of the late Duke of Orleans coming to light, and that it was not unreasonable, indeed perhaps wise, to make her acquaintance.

In recent years Charles had suffered so many spectacular military defeats at the hands of the English, the prospect of being exiled in Spain or Scotland was a very real and depressing possibility. In these circumstances perhaps he hoped this Virgin from Lorraine might be more useful than the ordinary visionary. Though he was a devout Catholic himself, attending mass daily and punctilious in observing saints days, he was not prone to be impressed by people claiming to hear voices from Heaven. He may have thought it odd that Yolande seemed to think it was worth his while to add to this one's reputation by being formally presented in Court, but his Bonne Mère was obviously determined that she should be. There were times when he resisted her wishes, but this wasn't worth making a fuss about. The suggestion that he should take her into an embrasure where they could talk in private was really rather extraordinary. But then again, if his Bonne Mère wanted him to do it, he didn't mind.

After Jehanne's arrival there followed several lively dis-cussions in his Council – was she really a woman? Investi-

77

gation showed that she was. As to whether there should be a reception at Court of a peasant also caused quite a stir. Charles, preferring to seem reluctant, agreed with apparent unwillingness to follow the normal routine and send the 'master of requests', Simon Charles, to inquire what she wished to talk to the king about. Jehanne, ignorant of this being the normal procedure, and believing it was a device to prevent her audience with Charles, was so infuriated by his visit she was ready to throw him out of her room. However, he managed to pacify her and explained this always happened, and then learned that she had received from the Lord of Heaven the commandment to relieve Orleans and conduct the dauphin to Rheims for his anointing and coronation.

On his return to the Council there was astonishment at hearing the second aim, and a still more lively debate ensued about the holding of a reception, but the eloquence of the king's confessor finally convinced them that they should receive this envoy in case she really was sent by God to rescue the king.

Three days after their arrival in Chinon her reception was held in the great panelled hall of the chateau. It was ninety feet long and fifty feet wide, with an elaborate triple vaulted cylindrical wooden roof. The hall adjoined the royal apartments. Fine tapestries decorated the walls, and fifty torches shed their light on more than three hundred courtiers and their wives dressed in magnificent clothes and jewels. Charles of France plainly clad as usual in a green velvet suit belted at the waist, lounged negligently against the big fireplace amongst his favourites, nothing to suggest that he might be the king except his sulky expression and wretched physique.

Meanwhile Jehanne had fretted in a fury of impatience until quite late in the day, when at last the head of the king's household accompanied by his usual retinue of gentlemen came to her lodging and introduced the welcoming delegation. This was as distinguished as she could have wished, being led by a prince of the blood royal, Louis de Bourbon, Count of Vendome, with an escort of the kind usually reserved for the most illustrious of visitors.

They went on foot up the very steep incline to the castle which was close to where she was staying. People were getting tired of waiting for this shepherdess when at last the door was opened to reveal the tall figure of the prince and the nearly as tall but disappointing figure standing beside him.

'But it's a boy!' nearly everyone exclaimed.

She did indeed look like a boy, a page, slim in her dark grey tunic with its leather belt, black hose and shoes with spurs. Her blue-black hair was entirely covered with a hood, her face weather-beaten. For a moment she stood scrutinising without embarrassment the crowd of haughty-looking people all staring at her, searching for the Dauphin. Then finding she was unable to pick him out, asked Vendome under her breath where he was, but before he could answer she caught sight of him, and immediately left her companions to stride unhesitatingly towards him. When three paces away from Charles she stopped, removed her hood and 'made the customary inclinations and reverences that people made to kings as though she had lived in a court all her life.'

'May God grant you a long life, noble Dauphin!' she greeted him, in her clear musical treble voice.

She spoke in perfect French! Surely a peasant would only know her Barrois patois, or even that ghastly Germanic dialect they spoke in Lorraine? And she had the nerve to deprive the king of his proper title!

Charles asked her her name and she answered, 'I am called Jehanne la Pucelle.' Next he asked her age and she answered, 'Three times seven.' She followed by volunteering the information that the Lord in Heaven had ordered her to raise the siege of Orleans and arrange his anointing and coronation in Rheims.

Charles then ushered her into an embrasure, where everyone could see them, but nothing could be heard. The onlookers could at least gauge the vicissitudes of the conversation, and these have been vividly recorded by a contemporary – Alain Chartier – who witnessed it.[12]

I quote his words in italics as I believe they reveal what Jehanne was talking about at that time to Charles. But before I begin, it is necessary to remember that ever since Jehanne had heard the Voice in the Garden when she was thirteen, she had been obliged to keep that experience and her visions a secret from everybody. The king and the Duke of Orleans were the only people she was allowed to tell. Now at long last she could

79

divulge everything. I imagine she could hardly wait to begin.

> *'Jehanne and the king began by an exchange of a few words which seemed to be civilities, then she seemed to be asking for permission to tell him something. The king inclined his head and the Maid began a long recital. At the beginning the king's face merely showed a polite attention, then a shade of astonishment passed over his features. He asked a question to which she responded with great heat. Charles VII smiled with some incredulity, while continuing to listen to the Maid's narration, which continued for a very considerable time. It appeared to the courtiers that the king even stifled a slight yawn.*
>
> *Then the Maid stopped and the courtiers supposed that the interview was at an end. But Jehanne began to speak again, slowly this time, and after her first words the king showed a lively emotion.'*

I believe this was when she told him that they were full brother and sister, with the same deplorable mother and romantic father. He had always been bitterly aware of the fact that his mother had absolutely no affection for him and Jehanne probably told him some of her early difficulties when she expected she would have to take the veil, and knew that she was adopted, but no one would tell her who she really was.[13]

> *'At a certain moment he interrupted Jehanne and asked a question with an air of great anxiety. And as Jehanne responded the witnesses were dumbfounded to see the king's face suddenly flooded with tears. Some of the men advanced towards him, but he gestured to them to stay away, and continued this extraordinary interview.'*

Without doubt the king's 'great anxiety' was due to his persistent doubts about the effect of his illegitimacy on his right to the throne. The time had now arrived when Jehanne had to reveal to the king the all important and dangerous secret she had learned in Lorraine. When she was able to assure him that it was quite immaterial who his real father was, he listened intently and when he was finally convinced, his relief brought him to tears.

> *'Now the king looked happy, joyous almost, and in his turn he talked to the Maid deeply moved.'*

I believe Jehanne then reminded the king that before it would be possible for them to solve all their problems in this way, they must carry out the commandment of the Lord of Heaven to have him crowned in Rheims. That was the most important thing for her to do. As soon as Orleans was in their hands they could turn their whole attention to that. And then I am sure she repeated that HIS CHILDREN WOULD HAVE MEROVINGIAN BLOOD IN THEIR VEINS, AND HIS SON WOULD BE THE FIRST RIGHTFUL FRENCH KING SINCE DAGOBERT II.

Finally she had the pleasure of telling him that the Third Order had collected enough money to pay for an army which would be able with her help to relieve Orleans and conquer the land as far as Rheims, provided they got there about St John's Day.

The interview lasted a good two hours. They ultimately left the embrasure and Charles called his chamberlain and told him to arrange accommodation for the Maid in the royal part of the castle, in the Caudray Tower. Within minutes Jehanne was being treated as though she were one of the highest people in the land – her domestic affairs looked after by the wife of the Duke of Orleans's personal secretary, two well-born pages appeared . . . and Jehan d'Aulon, the distinguished military expert, became head of her entourage. She was invited to attend mass in the king's chapel, and partake of his meals, and was free to enter his private apartments, which privileges aroused considerable annoyance and jealousy among many of the courtiers. She was provided with funds to replenish her wardrobe, and rejoiced in her sudden access to luxury. She chose expensive Flanders cloth in crimson and green – the Orleans colours. She had a new doublet and hose, and her green cape was embroidered with the white Orleans nettle leaves.

La Tremouille and Regnault de Chartres were particularly disturbed by the diminution of their influence over the king.

Jehanne and Charles spent a good deal of their time together in his rooms. One day a handsome young man entered unannounced and she asked who it was.

The famous military expert Jehan d'Aulon in the Caudray Tower.

'It's my cousin d'Alençon,' he replied.

At these words she got up and said enthusiastically

'You are very welcome! The more royal blood of France gets together the better!'

She was invited to stay at Alençon's castle with his wife and his mother, and the three women got on well together. Alençon had only recently been ransomed, having been taken prisoner at Verneuil, and his young wife – the daughter of the Duke of Orleans – asked Jehanne to look after her husband in any future battles.

'Don't you worry, I'll bring him back safe and sound to you!' she assured her.

Soon after her installation in the Caudray Tower an extraordinary scene took place, described both by her chaplain Pasquerel and in a book which has received the imprimatur (a licence to print) of the Roman Catholic Church. Jehanne walked into a room in Charles's quarters

82

where he and d'Alençon were conferring together with La Tremouille. Interrupting them she insisted that the king should renounce his kingdom in her favour. Charles didn't know how to respond, but eventually he accepted her proposition and as she wished, summoned some notaries, and ordered them to bring writing materials with them.

'Oh you needn't be afraid,' she assured Charles. 'I shan't misuse it.'

Addressing the notaries she said: 'Write in the proper and accepted way that Charles de Valois has given me, Jehanne la Pucelle, the Kingdom of France.' The record was made there and then. It was read out loud before d'Alençon and La Tremouille, who were flabbergasted.

Pointing to the dauphin she said, 'There, gentlemen, is the poorest knight in the kingdom. But it would not please God if I kept for myself such a splendid gift. I am only a deputy of the Lord, of the King of Heaven.'

Then addressing the notaries she said, 'Now write this: Very willingly I put the kingdom into the hands of the Almighty, King of Kings, the Lord God.'

The further clause was written. She knelt and prayed; then stood up and said, 'In the name of God the Highest, the Lord King of Heaven, of Whom I, Jehanne la Pucelle am the humble messenger, I install Charles de Valois, son of Charles VI of the name, as the trustee of the Kingdom of France, to hold this kingdom in usufruct as the worthy deputy of the King of Heaven, who is the sole master and the sovereign possessor of this said kingdom.'

'Write this, notaries, and arrange for the signatures of the dauphin and these gentlemen as witnesses, before I sign it myself.'

The symbolism of this act was not lost on the witnesses. Divine intervention had been involved in the dauphin accepting the kingdom of France as a trustee. He could not abdicate it to the English or the Burgundians. Also it accepted the Franciscan view of kingship, and all the social changes that that implied.

8

Opposition

Jehanne soon confirmed – for one cannot believe Yolande had failed to warn her – that she had enemies at court. Chief amongst them were Georges de La Tremouille and Regnault de Chartres, the archbishop of Rheims. La Tremouille's elder brother Jehan was Burgundy's chamberlain, and they kept in close touch with each other. They all believed that they could improve their own and Burgundy's position by pandering to Charles's dislike and fear of Richemont, and they had consistently done their successful best to counter Yolande's wishes whenever possible. Recently the discord with Richemont had so deteriorated that there was virtually a state of civil war between him and the Court. Jehanne's arrival had been, I believe, an unpleasant surprise for La Tremouille and the archbishop, and the influence she immediately exerted over Charles was enough to alarm them seriously. So it was only to be expected that the question of Jehanne's *bona fides* would come up for discussion in the King's Council. How, they asked, could they be sure that her inspiration really did come from Heaven? The Antichrist was reputed to be born of the Devil in times of war, and it was most necessary to be careful to verify that Jehanne was really a good Christian and a virgin, (for all witches were notorious for having fornication with the Devil).

So Jehanne was told it was necessary for her to be examined by a commission of enquiry in Poitiers presided over by Regnault de Chartres, to make sure that her inspiration was really from Heaven and not to be attributed to witchcraft. Poitiers at that time served as the capital city of Charles VII. It boasted a university and the Parlement met there. Some

84

seventeen or eighteen theologians and canon lawyers were assembled for this inquiry and were joined by some of the members of the Parlement. The Holy Inquisition was represented by a Dominican monk called Turelure who sat with the president. Jehanne herself had to submit to another physical examination which was carried out by Yolande d'Anjou, assisted by Jeanne de Preuilly the wife of Jehan de Gaucourt, the king's chamberlain, and the wife of the Governor of Orleans. Yolande reported to the king that she and the other ladies had found Jehanne a true and intact virgin, without any sign of corruption or violence.

Jehanne, accompanied by the king, Queen Marie, Yolande d'Anjou, the Duke of Alençon, Jean de Metz, Bertrand de Poulengy, and several other gentlemen, travelled to Poitiers where she was housed in the Hôtel de la Rose, the residence of the king's advocate general, Jean Rabateau, who was also the Duke of Orleans's counsellor.

Contrary to normal procedure the inquiry was held in the Rabateau mansion, and Jehanne, consumed with impatience at these endless delays and refusals to believe she was simply telling the truth, demonstrated what is often described as arrogance in the way she dealt with her questioners. I am inclined to think rather that it was simply exasperation at what seemed to her the idiotic questions they kept asking her. One theologian who spoke with a marked provincial accent inquired what language Saint Michael used, and she answered 'French, but he spoke much better than you do.'

I think the fact was, she was terribly worried by the delays in sanctioning her attempt to relieve Orleans, let alone freeing the route to Rheims for Charles's all important coronation. Except for dictating a letter to the English threatening them with dire consequences if they did not forthwith return to their own country, most of her free time was spent in desperate prayers to God begging Him to send a sign to the dauphin to convince him that he must exert himself at once to provide her with the means of fighting the English. I do not believe that modern historians have appreciated that she had another important hallucination while she was in Poitiers. She believed her prayers were answered when an angel appeared with a wonderful golden crown. He offered this to Regnault de Chartres who handed it to Charles. The angel told him it was a sign that he would rule over the whole of France quite soon, if only he would start at once to collect men-at-arms for Jehanne, otherwise it might be years before it happened. When she asked (the hallucinatory) Charles if he had been convinced by what the angel said, he said yes, he had been. This and subsequent events confirmed this and abolished her fears. She also believed that the archbishop and some other people standing near had experienced this vision and that hundreds of other people had seen the crown, subsequently taken away to be safeguarded in the king's treasury.

One can suppose that Yolande shared Jehanne's impatience with the refusal of the Commission to believe in the reality of her visions and voices. The objections raised in the Commission seemed without end, and finally Charles, doubtless incited by Yolande, insisted that two Franciscan monks be sent off by the Commission, ostensibly to Domremy and Vaucouleurs, to inquire about Jehanne's childhood. In fact the monks could never have travelled there and back in the time at their disposal. It seems they really went to Lyons and contacted Jean Gerson, the most revered of theologians and late chancellor of the University of Paris. He was one of Yolande's earliest collaborators. The attitude of the members of the Commission changed at once when they had read the report the monks brought back. It has not been officially revealed, but in fact it divulged who Jehanne's real parents were. Some people are satisfied by the suggestion that Gerson merely said that so many unlikely things had made it possible for her to come to Chinon, that one could only suppose it MUST be the will of God!

The arrival of the report and the visit of the angel seem to have happened about the same time. An important change occurred – the Commission stopped pestering her with silly questions. And then she learned the Court was shortly going to Tours to prepare for the campaign to free Orleans. All this convinced Jehanne that Charles really had taken the angel's 'sign' seriously and subsequent events confirmed her belief. Even though she was probably informed about the contents of Gerson's report, she would have given far more weight to her vision. The report would simply have been part of God's way of answering her prayers. A record of the Commission's investigation – their questions and her answers – was written in Rabateau's residence and became known as the *Livre de Poitiers*. It was never published, nor were any quotations given from it. Yet it is certain that it contained information that compelled the Commission, whose members had previously been at odds with one another and with Jehanne, to agree to give her its confidence and support, for no one of Royal Blood could conceivably be a witch.[13]

The conclusions of the Commission were sent to Charles VII between the 8th and 10th of April: 'The king, having regard to the need of himself and the kingdom . . . should not dismiss and reject the Maid who says she has been sent by God, even though her promises are only for human activities; nor ought he to believe in them forthwith and too easily.'

She returned to Chinon but soon left for Tours where her household, arranged by the king's chamberlain, was set up in accommodation provided by one of Yolande's advisors, Jehan de Puy. Her domestic affairs were entrusted to Anne de Maillé, the wife of Guillaume de Bellier, who had recently returned from England where he had been conferring with the Duke of Orleans. Jehanne had her own chaplain, Jean Pasquerel, and two well-born pages Louis de Coutes and Raymond. Her old friends Novelonpont and Poulengy were appointed her equerries, and her two foster brothers, Pierre and Jean Darc joined them. One of Yolande's most valued confidants, Jean d'Aulon, a distinguished military expert, one time a bodyguard of Charles VI, remained her chief of staff. Like a royal personage, she was provided with two heralds, Ambleville and Guyenne. Finally two cousins of the Darcs, Jean and Nicholas de Vouton, the latter a monk from the Abbey of Chaminon near Sermaize, who could deputise for Pasquerel, completed her household.

Jehanne had three ensigns, a standard, a banner and a pennon, the first and last made while she was in Tours, the banner may have been made in Blois. Her standard was shaped like a scalene triangle, two feet wide where it joined the staff and more than six feet long. It was white and probably made of linen. On one side a Scottish artist, Hamish Power, painted in oils the figure of God enthroned in the clouds, holding in his right hand the globe of the world, and near him were kneeling figures of Saint Michael and Saint Gabriel each holding a fleur-de-lis. Towards the point of the flag was the

Franciscan device of their three crosses and the words Jhesus-Maria, written in gold leaf. There were small fleurs-de-lis decorating the field. On the other side of the standard Hamish had painted an azure shield bearing the French coat of arms supported by two angels. Guérillon says there was a red dove too, its beak holding a wide red ribbon with the legend 'in the name of the King of Heaven' on it. The two painted pieces of material were separated by a fustian lining – a strong fabric woven of mixed cotton and wool, having a short nap. The standard was fringed, probably with alternate square pieces of white and gold silk.

Her pennon was about eighteen inches square. It was white silk and bore a picture of the Annunciation, showing a kneeling angel presenting a fleur-de-lis to Our Lady. This was burned accidentally soon after she arrived in Orleans, and was not replaced. These two ensigns cost twenty-five *livres tournois.* Jehanne was instructed by her saints what was to be represented on her ensigns and they evoked a lot of comment, not all of it favourable. Her banner just showed a crucifix, and was accepted without difficulty. It was normally carried by the clergy accompanying the army.

Guérillon has discovered an extremely interesting fact. In those days if the standards of noble families were flying unfurled and the king appeared, they all had to roll their flags up, and wait for the royal permission before unfurling them again. When Jehanne was about and the king appeared, her standard remained unfurled.

Her suit of white armour was made locally, possibly by someone expert in fashioning armour for horses, for most armour worn by men in those days was made in Milan. Hers was fabulously expensive, costing a hundred livres tournais; (Charles, Duke of Orleans had spent eighty-three livres on his.) It certainly was magnificent. Inlaid with gold and silver, it looked splendid when she sat on her black destrier, but it was, unfortunately, much too light to offer adequate protection in battle.

While she was in Tours her father's sword was fetched from Sainte-Catherine-de-Fierbois. Characteristically this incident was invested with a propaganda value, since it became generally believed that she had learned of the whereabouts of this sword through her Voices. She was presented with two scabbards, one made of crimson velvet and the other of fine cloth of gold. She herself had one made of strong leather. In addition she had a silver hatchet decorated with her crowned initial J, and her equipment was completed by golden spurs given her by Charles when she left Chinon, which were only worn by knights of high rank. He said as she left him,

'O Dieu du Ciel, par votre puissance
Conduisez donc la très noble Pucelle.'

'Oh God of Heaven, through your power
Guide henceforth our very noble Maid.'

Jehanne left Tours on April 22nd and went to Blois, where she met the king's army which was assembled there. At the same time what might be called the Joan of Arc Epic received another contribution throughout France – in Lorraine, in the Dauphiné, in Alsace, in the North, in Brittany, and even in Mainz – the following text was found:

'A virgin, whose limbs are dressed in male clothes, proposes because of an order from God, to restore the king of the fleur-de-lis to the rights of which he has been deprived, and will destroy his disastrous and impious enemies, in particular those who are at present encircling and crushing the city of Orleans by their siege. And if there are men plucky enough to join in this war and follow the army the White Maid is now preparing, you can rely upon the perfidious English succumbing . . . because the French will crush them with this feminine Mars. This will bring about the end of the war. Then the old alliance will be restored. And for this reason the English enemies, wearing the leopard, will not dare to call themselves kings of France.'

Yolande and Machet are credited with composing and distributing this manifesto.

There is a general tendency to suppose that before Jehanne appeared on the scene that the English had a widespread and firm grip on the territories which they had conquered. In fact it depended very much on whether they were urban or rural. The English regent had the real backing of people in Paris and several other towns, who approved of his relatively liberal approach to the University of Paris, the legal profession's organization and the craftsmen's guilds. But in the countryside a great many landowners had retained their loyalty to Charles and lived in exile rather then submit to the English. Their titles and estates were handed over to English heads of garrisons, on the understanding that they remained permanently in France and kept their area under control. The surrounding district was taxed by the English government to provide for the upkeep of the garrisons, but the payments were often barely large enough to be adequate, particularly if the French families had been popular. In general the English were greatly disliked. Burgundian territory was entirely under the control of the Burgundians and the English had virtually no influence there.

Bedford had disapproved of the plan to invest Orleans, wishing rather to attack Angers, but he had been overruled by the other English commanders. The French forces and their Scottish allies a couple of years earlier had been trounced in a spectacular defeat by the English at Verneuil, and Bedford had hoped to assemble a new army to follow this victory up with the minimum of delay, but his brother, Gloucester, had diverted the forces that had been collected to fight a private war of his own against Burgundy in Flanders. This did nothing to cement the alliance between the English and the Burgundians.

Feudal traditions were fading in England by this time, but not in France, and there it was considered outrageous to attack a province whose head was held as a prisoner of war by the attacker. The Duke of Orleans himself vehemently protested. It was officially suggested that a solution satisfactory to both sides would be to declare Orleans neutral and temporarily governed by the duke of Burgundy. Bedford who had little trust in Burgundy's integrity refused point blank, whereupon Burgundy withdrew all his men in the vicinity of Orleans and the surrounding countryside.

During April Yolande went to Blois, where she had arranged that the distinguished 'White Maid's Army' was to

90

assemble. Impressive quantities of provisions destined for the relief of the hungry inhabitants of Orleans were waiting there, ready for safe transport by the army. She had herself bought these, selling or pawning her jewels for the purpose. She had sent her messenger, Jehan Langlois, a citizen of Angers, to warn the Bastard that as many sailing ships as possible should be moored against the bank of the Loire opposite the Chécys Islands ready to transport the food with the minimum of delay when the army arrived with it. Arrangements were also made for its storage and safekeeping in the town. Langlois received ten gold crowns for his trouble.

Jehanne turned up with her entourage at Blois on April 22nd. While there it is likely that she ordered the white banner of white silk to be made, painted with a crucifixion, to be carried by the contingent of priests who would accompany the army. She made it abundantly clear that she expected everyone in the army to go to confession before he started, and the march began to the strains of 'Veni Creator', led by the priests who preceded them. Even Xaintrailles, a notorious roué, had confessed.

Jehanne's aims when she set out on her military career were firstly to relieve the city of Orleans, then enable the coronation of Charles to take place in Rheims. Next she would capture Paris thus restoring the real capital of France to Charles. Then in due course all the occupied territories would be liberated. During these activities she would capture as many English noblemen as possible in order to collect sufficient ransom money to liberate the Duke of Orleans. Finally a great crusade would be organized to liberate the Holy Land.

The position Jehanne occupied in the army is a matter of controversy. In a copy of a letter she wrote to Bedford, which was shown to her in Rouen, she describes herself as head of the army, but she denied she had ever described herself in this way. The fact remains that she was never invited to join the King's Council where strategy was discussed, and many historians, in the manner of many males before and since, systematically failed to give her any credit except as a lucky mascot. Yet the Orleans militia virtually refused to fight under anyone else, d'Alençon is known to have asked her what she wanted him to do, and she rather than d'Alençon was approached by Richemont when he turned up at a critical moment with his Bretons, ready to fight. The fact was, whatever her title, she was often in charge of affairs on the battlefield.

Maurice David-Darnac was an exception in that he regarded her as the finest military leader of the epoch. It must be admitted her fury at finding herself denied the opportunity of fighting the English the day the army left Blois for Orleans suggests that Yolande's strategy was much sounder than the Lord of Heaven's on that occasion. But after she was dead, many people who had fought alongside her, praised her skill in placing artillery, and in an extremely interesting account of various battles in which she played an active part – *Chronique de la Pucelle* – her tactical and strategic skill, it seems to me, is clearly demonstrated. No one denies her courage, nor her infectious enthusiasm, nor yet the way she led her troops from the front. And it must be noted that the French army suddenly enjoyed a series of victories instead of a nearly endless history of defeats. There were occasions too, when she failed to get the permission of the Dauphin to make some attack, and in spite of this she set out and came back to face him with a useful *fait accompli*. We should remember also, that she had a very demoralising effect upon the English soldiers who started to defect in large numbers, and recruitment in England became unusually difficult, admittedly because they thought she must be a witch. Would she have had that reputation unless she had been unpredictably victorious? The historic fact is that at numberless critical moments her inspiring leadership made all the difference between victory and defeat. Her formal title is of little importance.

Her initiative in making clear that she regarded Charles as a surrogate king of France for the King of Heaven, and the fact that her standard showed her identification with the Franciscans and Third Order, (who advocated social changes to benefit the poor at the expense of the aristocratic rich), added fuel to the antagonism in the King's Council against her.

At that time too there was bitter hostility between the Dominican and Franciscan orders, and their hatred was never far below the surface. The former who had instituted the Inquisition during the Albigensian Crusade and perpetuated it afterwards, were dominant in the University of Paris and generally supported the status quo. The Franciscan and Third Orders cherished Templar ideals and had the support of the poor clergy, the common people and the peasants. The threat Jehanne offered on this score was not lost on La Tremouille and his friends.

The fact that an army of some 7000 men had actually assembled at Blois was in the nature of a real victory for Yolande. The siege of Orleans had by then lasted some 200 days. The people who wished for the status quo to remain, however, comforted themselves when the great march began, because they judged the campaign would last another six months anyway, and a lot could happen in six months.

9

Liberation of Orleans

Marshall Boussac, Admiral Culant, Etienne de Vignolles known as La Hire, Marshall Saint-Sévères, Xaintrailles, Florents d'Illiers, Gilles de Rais, and many more people who trusted in the soundness of Yolande's judgment or had been inspired by her propaganda, came with their armed vassels and retainers. Robert de Baudricourt had come from Vaucouleurs. They were joined by some thousands of volunteers affiliated to the Third Order.

On the bright sunny morning of April 26th 1429 the great assemblage of some seven thousand men set out for Orleans with Jehanne at its head, her page Louis de Coutes beside her, proudly carrying her standard. Jehanne in her gleaming silver armour, with golden spurs and silver hatchet, riding her magnificent black charger felt quite certain, I am sure, that she was riding to victory.

Before long Gilles de Rais rode beside her, and a close friendship developed between them. He was an immensely rich man, and I believe he fell in love with her at first sight.

It was April 29th when it was announced that they had arrived at Orleans. Jehanne was dismayed and disgusted to discover that the city was on the other side of the river Loire and most of the English fortifications were there too. She had expected to have the opportunity of fighting the English, and was outraged at the safety-first tactics of the command. Naturally Yolande and the Bastard had had no intention of risking the safety of the valuable supplies they were delivering!

Jehanne rode down to the water's edge, infuriated at her

helplessness when she discovered how she had been, as it seemed to her, betrayed. There was no wind blowing and downstream she could see all the boats there, immobilized by the current, their sails hanging limp. D'Aulon and La Hire joined her. They saw a small boat being rowed against the current with very considerable difficulty. When it arrived a young man stepped out and greeted Jehanne:

'Noble Dame, comment vous va?' – 'Noble Lady, how are you?' It was an especially deferential form of address.

She looked at him, and apparently made it clear that she fully appreciated the difference in their social standing and answered:

'Are you the Bastard of Orleans?'

'Yes, I am. And I'm delighted that you have arrived.'

The Bastard of Orleans,
later ennobled as Count Dunois.

There then ensued an argument about the choice of route, which he defended. It left her unconvinced. 'In the name of God, the counsel of God our Lord is more trustworthy and wiser than yours. You have deceived me but further, you have deceived yourself, because I am bringing you the best help

95

that ever a captain or city has had: the help of the King of Heaven. Not for love of me, but for the pleasure of God Himself, who to please Saint Louis and Saint Charlemagne has taken pity on the town of Orleans, and He did not want to brook their enemies holding the lord of Orleans (the duke Charles) and his city.' With admirable tact he left her with the last word and suggested that perhaps she should return to Orleans with him, where a lot of people were waiting to see her, but she felt at first that she should not be separated from the army. Then, as probably happened every morning and evening about sunrise and sunset, the wind suddenly got up and now it blew upstream. The sails on the waiting boats billowed and they were able to get under way against the current loaded with Yolande's provisions. Of course the change in the wind was described as a miracle.[14]

Jehanne then realised how annoyed La Tremouille would be if she went back with the Bastard, so she accepted his invitation. After he had supervised the loading of the food, she with all the people who had been associated with her – Baudricourt, d'Aulon, her page with her pennon, Novelonpont and Poulengy, her two brothers and La Hire, were rowed across the Loire to the Burgundy Gate in Orleans.

It is interesting to learn that she ordered her chaplain and the priests to return with the army and carry her banner. This indicated to the initiated – English as well as French – that they were allies of the Third Order. Gilles de Rais led the army back to Blois where they picked up the other half of the provisions. They returned to Orleans on May 4th, by the same route, and then crossed to Orleans in the same way.

The Bastard took Jehanne carrying her pennon, her page and La Hire back with him to Orleans, the rest followed in another boat. When they arrived at the Burgundy Gate, they disembarked, walked over the drawbridge and arrived at the city, where they found horses ready for them. There was a white horse for Jehanne.

The time was about half past eight, and the Bastard had chosen it because it was dark, and he believed there would be few people about. There was, however, a considerable crowd, eager to enjoy the first glimpse of their liberator. Jehanne, giving her pennon to de Coutes who followed her, rode

The House of the Annunciation in Orleans where Jehanne stayed.

bareheaded beside the Bastard, her splendid white armour reflecting the light of the torches people were carrying. She surpassed their wildest hopes, it was obvious she was sent by Heaven to solve all their troubles. Everyone pressed forward to touch her and touch her horse, so their progress was slow, and later when they entered a narrow street, a shout of alarm went up as one of the torches set fire to her pennon. Jehanne looked back and seeing what had happened, showed her presence of mind, her horsemanship and her courage. Immediately rearing up her horse and wheeling it round, she extinguished the flames with her bare hands.

The crowd multiplied, men women and children, all deliriously happy, convinced they were about to witness the fulfilment of the prophesies they had long been told about. They surged around her all the way to the house of Jacques Boucher near the Regnart Gate, where she was to stay. Her host waited outside the House of the Annunciation to greet her, as he would do each time in the future when she came to the city. With him were his wife and ten-year-old daughter Charlotte. He was the treasurer of the Duke of Orleans and the most important of their citizens, handling all the duke's business and the financial affairs of Orleans. Although a bourgeois he boasted a coat-of-arms. It was he who furnished the Bastard with his annual income of a thousand *livres tournois* generously provided by his stepbrother the duke. If the king came to Orleans he too stayed at this house, the ducal palace having fallen into sad disrepair.

D'Aulon dismounted and helped Jehanne down from her horse. She looked worn out, and no wonder for it was the first time she had had her armour on for so long a time – since she had left Blois! And she had never faced such crowds. Her host approached her and said, perhaps because he was confused:

'Lady Jehanne, noble Princess, you are very welcome.' He bowed deeply several times. The Bastard, who had not dismounted, wished her goodbye and went off to his lodgings. Then she smiled at her hostess and kissed the little girl. The rest of her party were invited to supper and came in after her, d'Aulon, de Coutes, Bertrand de Poulengy, Jehan de Novelonpont, Robert de Baudricourt and her two 'brothers'.

Signature of Jehanne

Letter to the inhabitants of Riom
November 9th, 1429

She was courteously invited to occupy the place of honour at the table where they all sat down, but she was too tired to eat, and contented herself with a pint of wine, which she diluted with water, dropping a few pieces of bread into it. The rest of the party after a good meal, went off to their lodgings at the house of Thévenant Villedart de Bourges. Only d'Aulon and her page stayed with her in Boucher's house.

She was installed in two adjoining rooms on the first floor – a richly furnished reception room hung with tapestries and a bedroom. There was a bright fire burning in both rooms. Charlotte slept with her in a double bed, as was the custom, both of them being naked.

As usual Jehanne got up the next morning at seven o'clock and went to mass just across the garden in an ancient chapel, St Jean's, which pleased her very much. During the afternoon she visited the Bastard and had a long talk with him. She came back highly irritated, because he had decided they should wait for the army under Gilles de Rais to return from Blois before doing anything. However, he did allow her to write a letter to the English command which began by saying the Lord of Heaven ordered them to lift the siege against Orleans immediately, and finished with wild threats that unless they left the kingdom of France which they had no right to have invaded, she would wreak such destruction upon them that they would be astounded. The letter finished with the usual royal 'Because this is our pleasure.' Then came 'Jhesus-Maria' and on the line below, her signature. It was delivered by two heralds.

This was in accordance with chivalric practice, but it was a nicety not appreciated by the English, who retained one of the heralds and sent the other back with a rude note to the effect that surely she did not suppose they were going to give themselves up to a woman, but on the contrary they would burn her and the herald they had retained. They stigmatized this female who looked after cows as a whore of the Armagnacs.

The herald returned to the English with another note expressing disgust that they should treat heralds in this way. At once they released the herald they were holding.

The following day the Bastard decided to go to Blois, and elected to take d'Aulon with him, in spite of the fact that he certainly ought not to have left Jehanne alone. Perhaps it was because he believed she could not manage to put on her armour without him. But left to her own devices she got on her horse, and explored Orleans, attracting enormous crowds wherever she went, so that often she could barely move. When she returned to the House of the Annunciation the pressure the mob exerted on the door was so great that it cracked, and so she opened it and it was left open and a few people were allowed inside. Even though she was so approachable, her air of being a great lady led people to understand that she was closely related to the duke and a contemporary manuscript says that the people honoured her as though she had been the Duke Charles himself.

The second day she instituted a 'walkabout', entering simple people's houses, and toasting with their wine the end of the siege. (It is interesting to notice that 'toast', meaning a drink to celebrate, has been a French word since the fourteenth century.) One of the people she drank with in this way was called Jacquet Leprestre. He recorded the purchase of wine for la Pucelle many years later, after her 'execution'. To have had The Maid in one's own home, and to have chatted and drunk with her was a memory to boast about and never forget. That she was a most charismatic figure with a remarkable talent for inspiring a mob was demonstrated to the full, and her effect on the inhabitants of Orleans was immense and lasting.

On the third day she took part in a procession 'to implore Our Lord for the deliverance of this city of Orleans' – a further activity which added to the atmosphere of confidence that pervaded everywhere. For the rest she continued her walkabout.

May 4th saw the return of the army from Blois, with more supplies and a large increase in the number of volunteers. The same day the Saint-Loup fort was assaulted, and it is said that the tired troops had just sounded the retreat when Jehanne turned up and rallied them and the fort was overwhelmed.

When the English realized how great the reinforcements were, they stayed inside their other fortifications and did not let fly a single arrow even when some five hundred men under Florent d'Illiers came within their reach that evening.

It was not only amongst the French that the Franciscans

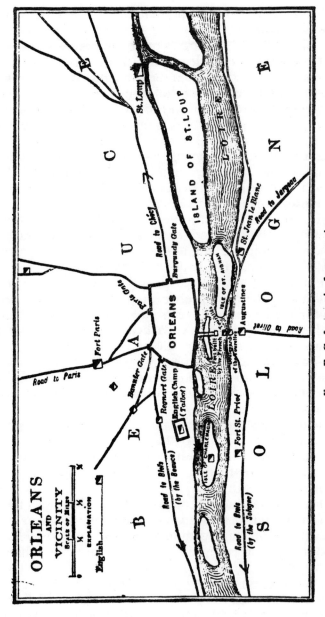

ORLEANS
AND
VICINITY

Scale of Miles

EXPLANATION

English

From F. C. Lowell's *Joan of Arc*.
By permission of Messrs. Houghton Mifflin Company.

with their radical social ideas were influential. The standard and banner associated with this army were by no means without effect. The Third Order was not confined to the French. The priests were never molested and this introduced a new and disturbing factor for the English to take into account, realizing as they now did that they were seriously outnumbered anyway. They had several different forts to man, and only some three thousand men could be deployed.

On the evening of May 4th the Bastard came to the House of the Annunciation and said that he had heard that Falstaff would shortly be arriving with reinforcements and supplies for the English. Jehanne exclaimed:

'Bastard! Bastard! I command you to let me know immediately when you know where he is – and if you don't I promise you I'll see you lose your head!'

He replied quite placidly that he would let her know as soon as he did, and went away.

The following day Gaucourt the governor called a meeting of the Bastard, the head of the volunteers and the captains of the militia, to discuss their plans. At the end Jehanne burst into the room and demanded to know what decisions had been taken. She was told they were to attack the fort of Saint-Laurent on the morrow in the morning. She replied, 'That's all right!' and added as she left the room, 'Provided that it's really carried out!'

That afternoon she wrote another letter to the English, saying:

'You Englishmen who have no right to be in the kingdom of France, are ordered by the King of Heaven, and I, Jehanne la Pucelle inform you of this, that you must leave your forts and return home. If you don't, I shall do such damage to you that you will never forget it.' She then had a proclamation read out in the city to the effect that no man-at-arms was to take part in the hostilities on the morrow until he had been to confession.

On May 6th, long after hostilities should have begun, nothing was happening. No orders had been given to the troops. So she decided to invite the militia to follow her in leaving the town. Soon the Bretons under Gilles de Rais, the mercenaries under La Hire, and 4000 soldiers of the royal

103

army elected to follow her. First they set fire to the fort that the English had abandoned the day before, then ran to the Augustinian monastery where the English were forced ultimately to retire, leaving many dead behind them. Jehanne mustered some of the soldiers near her and made a flank attack on the retreating English troops, throwing them into confusion so that they were unable to reach the fort. She and her men got there first, and standing on the parapet of the redoubt cried out, 'In God's name, come on!' The whole garrison was slaughtered. The building was then burned.

The troops were ordered to surround the next fort, the Tourelles, and to camp there to prevent reinforcements entering, but Jehanne who had hurt her foot in a trap earlier in the day went back to the Boucher house for the night – and this order was not adequately carried out. The English evacuated the fort of Saint-Privé and many of their men did get through to the Tourelles. As a result some 1200 men were there to protect it.

While she was having her supper a message arrived from Gaucourt saying there would be no hostilities the following day. The reason given was that the fact that the Tourelles were surrounded would seem they could safely wait for the arrival of new troops from the king. Jehanne replied, as might have been expected, 'You have your Counsel, and I have mine. You can believe that the counsel of my Lord will be followed, and yours will be ignored.' Then turning to Frère Pasquerel who was near her she added, without lowering her voice, 'Take care that you get up really early tomorrow morning. Do your best all the time to stay near me because I shall then be doing far better things than today!'

Soon after Gaucourt's messenger had left, a delegation of aldermen and citizens came to inform her that they were deeply worried by the announcement that operations against the English were to be suspended for some time. Jehanne cheered them up by assuring them that she was going to attack the Tourelles on the following day. She got up at three o'clock the next morning, May 7th. A considerable body of the militia was waiting for her and they rode to the Burgundy Gate to leave the town by the Faubourg Saint-Aignan. Arriving at the ramparts of the city she was confronted by Gaucourt surrounded by a detachment of the regular army. He explained he was there to prevent her passage because the Council had given the order that all military action was to be suspended. Jehanne interrupted him by saying, 'You are a wicked man to prevent my men leaving. Whether you want them to go or not, they are going!' At that moment the crowd of Jehanne's supporters started shouting, and Gaucourt, feeling a certain uneasiness infecting his men, hesitated. Jehanne, getting characteristically exasperated was unwilling to listen further. 'In the name of God, I'm going! Whoever loves me will follow me!' And surrounded by her militia she rode towards the gate. The governor, in spite of his rage opened it, sensing that otherwise he might well be killed.

The combat lasted all day. Four assaults were made during the morning, which were driven back and resulted in heavy losses. Early in the afternoon Jehanne made use of a ladder in an attempt to scale a wall, but she was shot at short range by a bolt from a crossbow which entered her neck, pierced her breastplate, and traversed her shoulder. She was taken from the field of battle by d'Aulon. After her wound was dressed she rested for a short while then returned to the Tourelles. It was beginning to get dark and she was just in time to prevent the captains sounding the retreat. 'In God's name, without a doubt we shall be going in there soon!' she assured them.

She rode at a furious speed towards the foot of the ramparts and stopped there, dangling her standard over the top. Nobody grasped it. 'Quick! Come here! It's all yours!' Her men rushed up the embankment and the English soldiers surprised by so unexpected a counterattack, rushed over the drawbridge. This had been undermined by fire and collapsed under their weight. Among the victims who were drowned was Glansdale, their commander, weighed down by his heavy armour. Before long the English, demoralised by the loss of their leader, and attacked on all sides, gave up and many were taken prisoner.

On the morning of Sunday May 8th Talbot and Suffolk collected all their fit men at arms from the forts on the left bank of the Loire still under their control and arranged them in order of battle not far from the city's walls. This stratagem had proved immensely successful in the past. Soon after Jehanne saw French regular troops coming out of the city, and realized that they would shortly be waiting for orders to attack the English. She was alarmed, because there was such an unqualified euphoria about everyone but herself, as a result of their recent victories. She realized the siege of Orleans was by no means over. If a new battle were now to end in defeat, yesterday's successes would count for nothing, and the army that had been assembled might well melt away with no chance of it reappearing.

One wonders if her solution was her own or her saints! She ordered that an altar should immediately be set up before the troops. No one dared to contradict her. Soon the priests were ordered to start singing hymns, responses and sacred orisons. Then two masses were said, followed by communion, taken by many of the congregation. By this time the English were deeply puzzled by this unusual response to an invitation to a battle, and possibly suspecting some dastardly ruse, decided to beat a retreat. They left behind in their forts their sick and wounded, considerable supplies, as well as the prisoners they had taken, and even some artillery.

'Let them go,' Jehanne said to the men who wanted to go after them. 'You will have another chance later on. Anyway, the Lord of Heaven does not want us to fight today.'

By the evening of May 8th, the Maid had completed the first part of her mission. It had taken nine days, not the expected six months to relieve the city.

On May 10th the king sent to all his 'Good Towns' a circular letter announcing the lifting of the siege of Orleans. After having detailed the various stages of the battle it added 'The Maid was always present in person at the execution of these events.' One suspects Yolande's hand in drafting this letter and arranging for its dissemination.

The joyous inhabitants of Orleans showered Jehanne with gifts – a beautifully worked saddle, some exquisite fabric for making a dress, and barrels of fine wines. The Duke of Orleans when he heard the news ordered his treasurer to spend 12 golden crowns to provide her with a splendid crimson dress and dark green cape with a border of white satin nettle leaves – the exclusive Orleans colours, her own colours.

In spite of her painful shoulder she left the city on May 10th to go to Chinon, because the mercenaries were not being paid and she had to get that put right. She reached Blois that

106

evening and the following day arrived in Tours. In the afternoon of 13th on the way to Chinon she met the Dauphin who had come to meet her, to show publicly how highly he regarded her. They entered Chinon together, riding side by side, Charles quite radiant, the Maid was said to be proud and gracious.

I do not believe she was proud. But I do believe she was filled with a sense of joy in the achievement, and gratefulness that SHE had been chosen to prove that if you really get your troops to trust in God and strive to the uttermost to do His bidding, He would give you the victory, He would make you victorious. It was the first step towards building the Kingdom of Heaven on Earth.

David-Darnac says she may well have expected her success to have improved her standing in the King's Council, but it only exacerbated the hostility with which La Tremouille and Regnault de Chartres regarded her. To stabilize Charles's position and finish the war was the last situation they wanted to see.

Jehanne was anxious to get the army setting out for Rheims without delay, only to find they advanced all kinds of reasons for postponing it. They said the country was infested with the English and Burgundians; new subsidies would have to be raised; it would be necessary to add to the army's weaponry; and Charles would never find such a good opportunity as now to make a definitive accord with the Duke of Burgundy. D'Alençon favoured recovering Normandy first, (his duchy was there). Only the Bastard, Dunois now ennobled, supported Jehanne's plan to drive the English from the banks of the Loire. He argued they were the places the English had been in for the shortest time and it would be necessary to clear them out before it would be safe to try recovering other parts of the country. This argument finally won the day, and the army was told to reassemble on June 5th at Scelles-en-Berry. The commander of the troops La Tremouille and Regnault de Chartres suggested should be d'Alençon, and this was agreed. He immediately said he wanted the Maid to accompany the expedition, a suggestion no one dared oppose.

Perhaps in the hope of reducing Jehanne's bitterness because she had not been appointed commander or admitted to the King's Council, Charles granted her a coat of arms. By

107

The Brevet dated June 2nd 1429 authorising Jehanne la Pucelle personally to carry the Royal Arms of France where the third Fleur-de-lis is replaced by a vertical sword penetrating the Dauphin's Crown. The colours are those of the Orleans Family an act dated June 2nd 1429, he authorised her personally, Jehanne la Pucelle, to carry the Royal Arms of France in which the third fleur-de-lis was replaced by a vertical sword penetrating the Dauphin's crown. The colours were those of the Orleans family. Although it was expressly stated that this could be carried on her standard, she never made use of it during this period. The brevet bestowing it was not discovered for a century or more. (It is now in the Bibliothèque Nationale, manuscript No. 5524).

Her disappointment in not being awarded command of the army was assuaged to some extent by both herself and d'Alençon equally having 'charge of the siege of Jargeau', a deliberately imprecise term.

When the English retreated from Orleans they reinforced the garrisons of three places that they had held for some time – Jargeau, Meung and Beaugency, and intended to remain there until Falstaff arrived with the reinforcements he had rushed to Normandy to collect. Scelles-en-Berry where the French army was due to assemble, was three or four days march from these places. Again Jehanne's opponents supposed it would take months to clear the Loire valley, giving them time to restore their influence over Charles and renew negotiations with Burgundy. But such a wave of enthusiasm had swept over the country following the liberation of Orleans, that more than 1200 lances assembled in Scelles as soon as the king's order had been learned. A lance normally consisted of ten armed horsemen and as many foot soldiers, all of them obeying their own commander, who would be made privy to the plans of the generals. A considerable number of mercenaries turned up as well.

As soon as the campaign had been agreed Jehanne went to Scelles. She arrived there on June 2nd. While she was there she sent the widow of du Guesclin, Anne de Laval, a gold ring. By this gesture she publicly announced that this new expedition was being placed under the patronage of the late Constable of France, who in the time of Charles V had vigorously – and successfully fought the English. He had also been the clandestine Grand Master of the Templars. And Jehanne made no secret of the fact that immediately after the coronation of Charles she intended to liberate Paris.

On the morning of June 8th the army left Scelles and

gathered under the walls of Orleans. The same day Falstaff at the head of 5000 men left Paris for the Loire. On 10th, Jehanne and most of the army made for Jargeau, and Dunois and Florent D'Illiers added their contingents from Orleans. This gave them such an enormous preponderance of numbers – the English had some seven or eight hundred men – the result appeared a foregone conclusion. But Suffolk had taken what precautions he could and concentrated all the artillery at his disposal against the French. In accordance with normal medieval practice the heads of the French army, the Bastard, Marshall de Broussac, Graville who was in charge of the crossbowmen, Admiral de Culant and others, discussed with Suffolk and his captains, a possible amicable agreement. It appeared then that La Tremouille and his associates had primed some of these gentlemen to adopt delaying tactics. Jehanne withstood these temporisers, arguing that 'God is leading this work'. D'Alençon did not dare contradict. So an assault was decided upon, and the army got under way.

Suffolk boldly tried to break the attack. After an initial bombardment of the troops a contingent of English soldiers rushed out and caused tremendous disorder among the French who then retired. Every hour that passed seemed to show that the English would be able to hold out until Falstaff arrived. Jehanne then showed her remarkable originality as a strategist. She insisted that all the artillery in Orleans should be dismounted and brought to Jargeau, and it was re-assembled there. Meanwhile waving her standard she rallied a number of the retreating troops and initiated a violent counterattack which succeeded in establishing themselves in the streets outside the walls of the town where they spent the night.

On the morning of June 12th Jehanne ordered that all the cannon should be fired simultaneously at the old tower of the castle which very quickly collapsed. During this bombardment the heads of the army were conferring together and coming to no useful conclusions. Things were much complicated because it was discovered that La Hire had offered Suffolk that if he would retire he would be paid a certain sum of money, to which he had replied that he suggested a truce of fifteen days followed by a rendering of accounts. Such an approach was not normal practice, and the manoeuvre caused a lot of discontent among those to whom it was news. The situation was later resolved because Suffolk decided to turn the whole idea down.

Jehanne profited by the bad tempered conference. Without even asking for d'Alençon's opinion, she ordered an immediate attack on the fortress. When he discovered this he said that he thought it was premature, to which she replied, 'Come on noble duke! To the assault!' And when he still hesitated she said, 'Ah noble duke, are you afraid? Didn't you know that I promised your wife that I'd bring you back safe and sound?' Piqued and possibly reassured he joined the battle. It lasted four hours, by which time the attackers were beginning to show signs of exhaustion. Jehanne went down into the ditch and put a ladder against the wall and began to mount it. She had nearly reached the top and was able to look through a breach in the wall, and saw it was unguarded beyond. Suddenly an avalanche of stones tumbled over her, knocking her down to the ground. The staff of her standard was broken. But she was protected by her metal helmet and armour and shouted, 'Go up! Go through the hole! There's no one there!' The English, taken unexpectedly in the rear, were at last overcome.

During the evening of this Sunday June 12th 1420 Jehanne returned to Orleans which gave her a wildly triumphant welcome.

10

Rheims and the Coronation

Jehanne left Orleans on June 15th. This time there was little objection to mopping up that part of the Loire district, Meung and Beaugency, whose garrisons were commanded by Talbot. The royal army replaced the losses it had sustained at Jargeau by a number of small units which turned up spontaneously, led by the Count of Vendome, Gilles de Rais, the young Guy and André de Laval (grandsons of du Guesclin), and a number of other notables, to say nothing of more mercenaries.

Talbot decided that the troops at Meung should be reduced to be sufficient only to hold the fortress, as he did not believe he could withstand a full assault with the troops at present at his disposal. With some forty lances he marched north to Beaugency, where he made the same arrangement, leaving Richard Guétin, the bailiff of Evreux in command. He then made for Janville to meet Falstaff.

At the beginning of the first afternoon the vanguard of Charles's troops captured the fortified bridge at Meung, thereby protecting the flank of the bulk of the army advancing towards Beaugency. The garrison retired to the fortress. On the morrow Charles's army entered Beaugency with little difficulty, the English forces also retreating into their fortress at the first assault. Jehanne immediately surrounded it by a solid cordon of soldiers. There was no call to attack it at once on account of two unexpected pieces of news brought by a couple of envoys, the Lords de Rostrenem and Tugdual de Kermoisan. They came to say that the Constable Arthur de Richemont had decided to take part in the siege of Beaugency and then added for good measure that Talbot had joined Falstaff at Janville – which, of course, presaged an imminent attack by the English. D'Alençon immediately told Jehanne that if Richemont turned up he would not hesitate to attack him, since he and La Tremouille had signed an undertaking promising Charles to fight him if such a situation ever arose. Highly displeased with this unexpected contretemps, just at the time when the English were in a position to take the offensive, Jehanne tried her best to persuade d'Alençon to change his mind, whereupon he said Jehanne could choose between them. If Richemont was coming, he was going to leave. In order to quieten him, she pretended to give way, but when they were told about the situation La Hire, Gilles de Rais, Girard de la Paglière and other captains warned them that if there were to be a fight between d'Alençon and Richemont, they would all be on Richemont's side. D'Alençon thought better of it.

Meanwhile in Janville Falstaff and Talbot were arguing about their plans. Falstaff deplored the way the English forces had been divided into so many parts, and argued that they should concentrate all their troops in a few places far to the north of the Loire. There they could safely await the arrival of large reinforcements from Bedford, and then make an assault with a real chance of success. Talbot thirsting to have his revenge on the Maid, refused to listen to this sound plan. By the evening of June 16th Falstaff acceded with a bad grace to meet the French forces as Talbot wished.

On June 17th Richemont turned up before Beaugency with a force of some 8000 Bretons – about 400 lances and 800 archers. At the same moment the French lookout warned that the English forces had come into view. It was a tense situation, emotions were high and the least incident could have sparked off a fight between the French and the Bretons. Jehanne did not hesitate. Doubtless aware that Yolande would rejoice in and approve of her action, she approached Richemont and dismounted. The constable immediately riding towards her, dismounted in his turn. He put his point of view with admirable brevity.

'Jehanne, people have told me that you want to fight me. I don't know whether you are for God or not. If you are, I have no reason to be afraid of you, because God knows my good intentions. If you are for the devil, I fear you even less!'

David-Darnac points out that Richemont obviously

Arthur de Richemont, Constable of France.

regarded Jehanne as being in charge of the French army, 'you want to fight me', and he follows this by suggesting two double entendres, the first 'God knows my good intentions', reminding her that he had sworn a vow of lifelong loyalty to the king, which he never had and never would violate. The second, 'if you are for the devil' this could evidently apply to La Tremouille who had treated him so shabbily, and was behaving in the same way towards Jehanne herself.

Jehanne answered: 'Good Constable, you haven't come for

my sake, but you have come and you are very welcome'.

He then asked her to try to get the king to restore him to favour, and Jehanne immediately promised to do her best. D'Alençon seeing how things had gone made no objection, and was doubtless glad that the responsibility was wholly Jehanne's. The Maid showed her good sense in assigning Richemont to guard the bridge at Beaugency while the French army should take up battle positions in front of Meung. In this way trouble between the two armies was avoided.

During the evening emissaries were sent to the French command by the English to offer battle. Jehanne's reply surprised them. She said it was too late to start fighting today, but that she would fight tomorrow and offer no quarter. This was gladly accepted by Falstaff as his troops were tired after their long and hurried march, and they retired towards Meung to spend the night. Jehanne had a good reason for suggesting this postponement. She had promised Richard Guétin, commandant of the garrison at Beaugency to choose whether they would freely evacuate the fort by dawn the next day or face no quarter if the French assault succeeded. If they left, they would swear not to fight for the next ten days. Having seen Talbot and his men depart without a fight he supposed he had been abandoned, and chose the former alternative. He left very early the next morning with five hundred soldiers. When the English learned of this evacuation of Beaugency – the last place in the Loire where the English had any real support – Falstaff, ignoring the protestations of Talbot, insisted on the whole English force as well as the garrison at Meung, making for the north! As a result the whole valley of the Loire was cleared of the English.

Of course efforts were made by La Tremouille to prevent further progress towards Rheims saying it was necessary to wait for further instructions from the King's Council. The Maid circumvented these suggestions by ordering the French forces to pursue the enemy who were making for Etampes, the first step on the way to Paris. The English were advancing but slowly, partly because they had a lot of material to move, but also they were tired and the terrain was extremely difficult. In those days, the country known as the Beauce had not been drained and one kept coming across quagmires and almost impassable prickly thickets and dense coppices which might have been designed for ambuscades.

At the beginning of the afternoon of June 18th La Hire's scouts caught sight of the English rearguard who seemed to be trying to conceal themselves in some copses near the village of Patay. As soon as they were noticed Jehanne ordered the captain of her volunteers to circle wide around them and ride ahead with their cavalry so as to cut Falstaff's road to Paris and force them to fight. While they were going forward a stag appeared which excited all the English soldiers' dogs to give chase. It soon became apparent that the whole English force not merely the rearguard was there.

Everyone apparently including d'Alençon asked the Maid what they should do? To which she answered, 'Use your spurs!'

'What, take to our heels?'

She replied, 'NO! Fight them! They wont know how to defend themselves. You run over them! Use your spurs! In the name of God, you've got to fight them! God has sent us to punish them! The noble king will have his best victory yet today! My counsel tells me they will all be ours!'

The Maid quickly assigned particular tasks and positions to the various contingents. For instance La Hire was to provide a diversion by attacking the vanguard's flank. She and some of the other captains were to throw the rearguard into disorder and then charge into the centre. The bulk of Falstaff's army was thus cut into two, its vanguard encircled and its rearguard dispersed. They were so seriously outnumbered that they found themselves at the mercy of the French. Some five thousand prisoners were taken and as many men were killed. It was the first time since the Hundred Years War had begun that the French had had any such resounding success against the English in open country.

One detects La Tremouille's hand in the letter Charles sent to the Dauphiné: 'We inform you that yesterday, which was Saturday June 18th, our noble nephew d'Alençon and other lords and captains, and having with them the Maid . . . '

Pretending to believe that Charles was determined to be crowned in Rheims, Jehanne returned to Orleans and collected all the armed men and military material that she could lay hands on. Then she announced that the next army

116

should assemble in Gien. Three events, wholly unexpected by her enemies in the King's Council, ruined their plans. First a place called Bonny surrendered to Admiral de Culan, and then aristocrats, captains and ordinary folk flocked to Gien to enlist in Jehanne's army. Finally the Maid sent out 'on her own authority', (doubtless prompted by Yolande), letters announcing that Charles was going to be crowned in Rheims, and inviting the recipient of the letter to attend the ceremony!

Charles found himself obliged to concur, in spite of the efforts La Tremouille and Regnault made to persuade him that the march on Rheims should be postponed. He knew a refusal would make himself utterly ridiculous. There was so much enthusiasm for the coronation throughout the country that he really had no choice. The queen and Yolande were prevented from joining the expedition ostensibly on grounds of economy. Her enemies may have hoped that were Jehanne sufficiently isolated they might still get the better of her.

Meanwhile the Maid was consumed with impatience. After seemingly endless delays she decided to face Charles with another *fait accompli*. On June 27th she left Gien followed by the army and made camp four leagues before Montargis. By June 29th Charles came to the conclusion that he had to join her. The expedition could hardly be described as a simple route march! The royal army consisted of some 12,000 men and it was headed by experienced leaders – those who had been active in the Loire campaign – d'Alençon, the Bastard of Orleans, La Hire, Poton and others, and it was not exactly necessary to advance across provinces like Picardy, Champagne, Ile-de-France, Brie, Gatinais, Auxerois and Burgundy, all nominally occupied by Bedford's troops or under the control of Philippe of Burgundy.

Jehanne was fully aware that the English forces were in disarray, Burgundy had been dealt with by inviting him to the coronation, and letting it be known that he had been invited. It was hoped this might make certain municipalities uncertain whether it would be wise to refuse to receive Charles's soldiers.

On the morning of June 29th Saint-Fargeau welcomed the forces of the king of France. Late in the evening they arrived at Auxerre who replied to a request that they should open their gates that 'they did not care for either the Armagnacs nor the Maid'.

To this insolent reply Jehanne was all for making an immediate attack, in order to convince other cities that might be thinking of responding in the same way that it was altogether too big a risk to take. However, La Tremouille suddenly remembered that technically he was the Governor of Auxerre. Originally it had been part of Charles V's domain, but after the English had conquered it, they had given it to the Duke of Burgundy. In spite of Jehanne's strong disapproval and murmurs in the army, Charles accepted his favourite's proposal that the town should be spared if it declared itself neutral and provided the food required by the troops. The city also paid a plump sum – some two thousand crowns – to La Tremouille for his good offices!

This was a damaging precedent as it invited powerful cities on the way to Rheims to offer a lively resistance which could suggest grave reactions on the part of the Duke of Burgundy. And this was just what La Tremouille and Regnault de Chartres were praying for. As a kind of compromise a letter was sent on July 3rd to the inhabitants of Rheims, beginning with an account of the victories on the Loire, then informing them that Charles was on the way to the city in order that he should receive anointment and coronation there. And it added that the king would not remember any offences that might hitherto have been committed against him, but would regard them as loyal and good subjects and would be prepared to meet their deputies with great pleasure. Not even the name of the Maid was mentioned!

On July 4th the royal army entered Champagne. The English having insufficient forces to occupy this French province they had given the administration into the hands of influential Frenchmen sympathetic to their cause. The head of the local government was the Bishop of Beauvais, Pierre Cauchon.

Jehanne personally wrote a letter to Troyes, mentioning the troubles people would be involved in if they refused to receive the king, but assuring all loyal Frenchmen that their persons and goods would be safe otherwise. The letter was addressed to the 'Very dear and good friends, noblemen, citizens and inhabitants of Troyes.' This was in reply to a letter she had received from Jean Laiguisé the bishop of the town, delivered to her by a Grey Friar, called Brother Richard, asking what were her intentions.

An official letter from Charles was also sent the same day to the Council of Troyes, dictated by La Tremouille, demanding that the inhabitants should render obedience in receiving the king and saying there was no wish to exact vengeance, but on the contrary they wished past things to be forgotten. This letter was sent by two heralds. La Pucelle was not mentioned in it.

Jehanne's letter received no answer. To the dauphin the heralds brought back a verbal message that the inhabitants had promised Henry VI and Philippe le Bon to allow no force to enter the city which outnumbered the garrison left there by the English and Burgundians. At the same time Troyes wrote to Rheims telling it that they intended to resist Charles's army to the last man, and asking that the Dukes of Bedford and Burgundy be begged to send reinforcements to Troyes immediately. They also mentioned that they had received a ridiculous letter from Jehanne which had given them a good laugh, and they had thrown it on the fire without sending any reply.

The next day the French army arrived at Troyes and was met by a sortie which was so vigorously repulsed that the defenders had no choice but to retreat inside their walls. For several days the combatants consolidated their positions, and it looked as though there would be a long siege. The inhabitants were well provided with provisions, but Jehanne's army had experienced considerable hunger already, the food collected from Auxerre having mysteriously melted away. There was a real likelihood of reinforcements arriving from Bedford and Burgundy before long. In fact everything looked to be in favour of La Tremouille and Regnault de Chartres.

The king assembled his Council and asked what he should do in this situation. The Archbishop of Rheims immediately answered that he should retreat at once to the Loire, and this was supported by everyone except the former chancellor of the king, Robert de Maçon, one of Yolande's most loyal supporters. He maintained that the whole enterprise had been undertaken on the advice of the Maid, and that nothing should be done before consulting her. Almost as he finished speaking Jehanne burst into the place where they were holding the meeting, and asked if Charles would believe what she had to say? Unable to reply evasively to this question, she proceeded to assure him that if he would wait two or three days the town would obey him, 'either willingly or by force.'

Realising that the army would refuse to withdraw if this was Jehanne's opinion, it was agreed that they would not order a retreat at once. Then pointing to Regnault, in a voice full of resentment, she said, 'And that deceitful Burgundian will be greatly astonished!'

Regnault began to stutter that he was willing to wait ten days. Jehanne turned to the Dauphin and said that he could dismiss his Council.

'In the name of God, you'll have Troyes tomorrow!'

She immediately left and began preparations for an all-out assault on the town. By the following dawn the artillery was all in place, trenches had been dug where required, supplies distributed. The defenders on the walls watched all these preparations with growing alarm which spread to the whole populace. Bishop Laiguisé who was no supporter of the Burgundians, reminded people how armies pillaged when they had the chance, and Brother Richard, who was an experienced demagogue with Franciscan sympathies, let his imagination run riot and assured his hearers that Jehanne was quite capable of raising herself and her army up in the air, so they could come over the walls without waiting for the gates to be opened.

Meanwhile Bedford on June 29th realized that the provinces he occupied were facing a new order of threat. He sent the bailiff of Vermandois to Rheims to remind the inhabitants of the oath of loyalty they had sworn to Henry VI. He was accompanied by Pierre Cauchon, the Bishop of Beauvais, who was also an archdeacon of Rheims. They were honourably received by the citizens, but prudently – their escort was limited to four cavaliers. On July 10th Rheims Council was informed that the Duke of Burgundy would be unable to send any artillery help for some six or seven weeks, and at the same time they received letters from the towns which had surrendered peacefully to the royal army. They had all found the troops had behaved with the utmost correctness. Brother Richard too had come, reawakening the loyalist sentiments of the people and the lower ranks of the clergy.

While the bailiff of Vermandois tried without success to stem the course of events Cauchon, a past master at grasping the implications of the whole of a situation, counselled the local clergy not to oppose the entry of Charles into their city, and quietly disappeared before the arrival of his hierarchic superior Regnault de Chartres. It is important to remember that it would have been easy for him to confiscate the Holy Oil that was an essential adjunct to a coronation had he so wished.

On July 9th, Troyes decided that discretion really was the better part of valour, and accepted Jehanne's terms of surrender –. basically no looting on the part of the army, and the provision of food for her soldiers. During the afternoon Jehanne, who had so recently been described as ridiculous by their deputies, rode into the town saluted by the enthusiastic acclamations of the populace. On July 11th Charles and the Maid rode together amidst exuberant crowds, all the church bells ringing a welcome. For the first time since the march to Rheims had begun, the Dauphin looked happy, radiantly happy, this wonderful experience effacing the dreadful time when his mother in this city had pronounced him the so-called Dauphin, a bastard, and the shameful Treaty of Troyes had been signed.

The army continued its march to Rheims on July 14th. The example of Troyes had a tremendous effect on other places and Charles entered Chalons to a warm welcome. It had previously said it would resist to the death. This change was partly thanks to Brother Richard who had preceded the army and persuaded the citizens that they should open their gates, and for the rest it was due to their bishop Jean de Sarrebruck, a supporter of Yolande, who said he himself was going to meet the king, and did so with quite a crowd of the inhabitants. After the official ceremony of welcome, Jehanne received with unaffected friendliness and pleasure five people from Domremy who came to see this young woman from their village, who in less than six months had become renowned throughout France. In gratitude for their visit she gave them all presents.

The army arrived in Rheims in the afternoon of August 16th. Coronations had to take place on a Sunday, so to forestall any manoeuvres on the part of La Tremouille, Jehanne insisted that it take place on the morrow. One's heart quails at the thought of how many hurried makeshifts, substitutes and improvisations must have been necessary. But the Sacred Oil was irreplaceable. It was kept in the tomb of Saint Remi in an abbey miles away from Rheims. Gilles de Rais accompanied by his brother René de la Sieze, le Sire de Culant, Admiral of France, and le Sire de Graville, Grand Master of the Archers, rode through the night to fetch it, and returned with an abbot carrying it at half past nine the following morning. Charlemagne's Crown, the Staff of Justice, Saint Louis's Fastener, which were all part of the traditional accoutrements, were in the Abbey of Saint Denis in English hands. But a golden crown was found in the cathedral treasury, the six lay peers demanded by the Pontifical were mustered by assembling d'Alençon, the Counts Vendome and de Clermont, La Tremouille and the young Guy and André de Laval. The six ecclesiastical peers were more difficult to raise, as one should have been Cauchon, Bishop of Beauvais, so he was deputized by a canon of the cathedral. The Constable of France, Richemont, (still out of favour), was replaced by d'Albret, a half-brother of La Tremouille, and ironically enough, the ceremony was undertaken by Regnault de Chartres. He had been deprived of the possibility of functioning in his diocese for years, and now he found himself performing his first act as Archbishop of Rheims crowning Charles, able to officiate only because la Pucelle, whom he hated, had triumphed so spectacularly in spite of his best endeavours.

After Jehanne came into the Cathedral for the coronation, a murmur arose amongst the congregation when her standard was brought in. The sole standard normally present at a coronation was that of the French Royal Family. Hers was not even that of an aristocratic dynasty, but of the Franciscan Third Order – derived from the outlawed Templars. There is no written evidence that the presence of her banner was actually questioned at the time or that she answered 'It had suffered the pain, it is only right that it should enjoy the honour', but there is a tradition that she did say this. Later she certainly justified its presence in this way, when questioned about it in Rouen.

Another ironic anomaly at this coronation was the position Jehanne occupied in the cathedral – she stood next to the Dauphin. This place was the prerogative of the Dauphin's next of kin! Yet had the Duke of Orleans been present it would have been he who stood there, and d'Alençon, his cousin would have been his expected proxy.

For once Charles did not wear green but red velvet. Jehanne was dressed magnificently in cloth of gold and silk. When the ceremony was completed she was overcome by emotion and falling at the king's feet burst into tears and said:

'Noble king, the will of God has been fulfilled; He wanted you to come to Rheims for your rightful coronation to show that you are the true king, to whom the kingdom ought to belong.'

A few minutes later the Maid introduced a man from Metz. His name was Nicholas Louve. Jehanne told the king that Louve had come from Metz especially to see this coronation, and begged Charles to make it the most wonderful day in his life by making him a knight. This Charles consented to do. No one else was so honoured. Louve many years later became Charles's chief chamberlain.

I have no evidence to support my belief that Louve was so privileged because he had been responsible for collecting the funds from the Third Order which financed the army making this coronation possible, but it is a very reasonable proposition as he was an important member of the Third Order, as well as being a personage greatly respected in Lorraine. He later was appointed chamberlain not only to Charles, but also to the Holy Roman Emperor and the Duke of Burgundy.

There is only one document that mentions the name of Jacques Darc as being in Rheims at that time. Isabelle was not with him. He stayed at the inn of the *Ane rayé,* the Striped Ass, and he was there for a whole month, waiting it seems, for a royal order signed by Charles VII 'at the request of our beloved Jehanne la Pucelle to grant the villages of Greux and Domremy a complete remission of taxation.' This order was signed on July 31st 1429 at Chateau-Thierry, and it was sent, not to Rheims but to Chaumont, where the king of France's bailiff lived.

Jehanne left Rheims four days after her arrival, anxious immediately to fulfil her third aim – the conquest of Paris. But her enemies in the King's Council dangled a promise by the Duke of Burgundy to relinquish Paris without a fight in exchange for a treaty. Charles was persuaded to sign a fifteen day truce – which enabled Bedford to reinforce Paris with an army of more than ten thousand men. And the French army, instead of making for Paris was diverted through Soissons, Chateau-Thierry and Provins towards the banks of the Loire. Bedford, however, during the night of August 4th occupied the solid bridge which existed over the Seine at Bray, and withstood the assault of the vanguard of the French army. The retreat to the Loire thus being prevented unless Charles was prepared to fight a real battle, Jehanne persuaded him to make for Paris after all.

11

Eclipse and Capture

On August 10th they had reached Ferté-Milon and on 11th Crespy-en-Valois. From there the royal army did not reach the environs of Paris until September 7th, when Charles entered Saint-Denis.

This long delay was due to Bedford having sent 8000 men to Senlis, making the king think that he was liable to have his forces cut in two, but in fact Bedford withdrew his men without a fight. Doubtless La Tremouille was privy to this scheme.

When the fifteen day truce came to an end Philippe of course failed to carry out his part of the bargain. He did not hand over Paris as he had promised. Continuing his fruitful seesaw policy he accepted Bedford's suggestion that he become governor of Paris on behalf of Henry VI, and at the same time received a French deputation in Arras, headed by the Archbishop of Rheims, who proposed substantial advantages to Burgundy if he were to quit his alliance with the English.

On August 20th the archbishop returned with a Burgundian delegation to meet Charles who had just entered Compiegne. After a week of bogus negotiations, Charles quite fooled by his advisers, signed a second truce with Philippe to last until Christmas. Jehanne, exasperated by all these spurious transactions decided to repeat her policy which had succeeded so well at Gien, and face Charles with a *fait accompli.*

On August 23rd she said to d'Alençon: 'My good duke, get your men together and any of the other captains who would like to join us. I want to have a closer look at Paris.'

Three days later most of the royal army was camping at Saint-Denis. It looked as though the Maid was about to succeed. La Tremouille and Regnault de Chartres redoubled their efforts to keep Charles at Senlis until September 7th to allow the Duke of Luxembourg, Henry VI's chancellor, time to defend the capital which Bedford had abandoned, preferring to retreat to Rouen.

Jehanne prepared a bridge of barges to cross the moat, but the next morning she found it had been sabotaged. After fighting all day she was quite seriously wounded by an arrow which pierced her thigh. In vain she begged her captains to stay in front of the walls until morning, but helpless when she was absent from the field of battle, they retired to La Chapelle. The following day Jehanne gave the order to renew the attack, but just as it was getting under way, and they were unexpectedly reinforced by some sixty Armagnacs leaving the city who were prepared to join forces with them, René d'Anjou appeared with a formal order from Charles to stop fighting and return to Saint-Denis. In spite of this, Jehanne, still furious over Charles's order, told her captains that they would make a further attack the following dawn at another part of the city, but during the night another bridge hurriedly constructed by d'Alençon was destroyed by the order of the chamberlain and the chancellor. Jehanne returned to Saint-Denis and hung her armour and her sword *ex voto* in the chapel there. She was defeated.

The bottom had dropped out of Jehanne's world. She was no longer a factor in Yolande's plans. The conquest of Paris, the release of the Duke of Orleans, driving the English out of the rest of France and the glorious prospect of a crusade to liberate the Holy Land, had all crumbled into nothing. She was powerless to do anything about it. Fifteen days after the return from Paris the army had been disbanded, and when the captains and their troops had dispersed, Charles took to wandering indolently from one of his residences to another. It is easy to forget that Jehanne would still have been having her hallucinations, but whereas previously her Saints' views were normally backed up by Yolande, now she was virtually left on her own and no one else shared her burning sense of the importance of the other parts of her mission. D'Alençon returned to his place in Beaumont, and began collecting a certain number of men and materials with a view to winning back his land in Normandy from the English. When he asked that the Maid should go with him the request was decisively refused. She discovered she was effectively a prisoner in the Court, as she found his favourites had extracted from Charles that she should not be allowed to join up with d'Alençon. The last thing the chamberlain and chancellor wanted was a resounding victory against the English. Bored with luxury and the attentions of people she did not care about or actively disliked, she fumed over her everlasting inaction, and perhaps questioned why Heaven remained so uncooperative.

Her hopes were raised when she was invited to join in a limited military activity cleaning up various small pockets of enemy occupation in the upper reaches of the Loire. La Tremouille's half-brother d'Albret was made commander of a small force to do this. This arrangement had the advantage that should there be a victory, it could be credited to him, but a defeat might be attributed to her. And since she always tended to lead her troops from the front, the conspirators counted upon the dangers of war giving them a fair chance of eliminating Jehanne for good.

In early November a siege was begun of Saint-Pierre-de-Moustier. D'Albret at once demonstrated his total incapacity as a leader, and the royal troops' attack looked like turning into a shambles. Jehanne, stranded nearly alone in the vanguard, grasped the initiative and before long turned the tide and led the men in an irresistible assault.

Encouraged by this further demonstration of her military skill, she hoped the next offensive could be directed against the Ile-de-France or Normandy. But the King's Council decided otherwise and directed them to reduce La Charité-sur-Loire. Far too few in numbers, hardly armed and fed, the royal troops invested the place for more than a month, and then in some inexplicable manner that has never been cleared up, the artillery she had painstakingly managed to collect fell into the enemies' hands. A month later on January 11th 1430, the governor of the town elected to recognize the authority of the king of France provided that he was paid 1300 gold crowns to do so. He was paid.

For the rest of the first quarter of that year Jehanne lived in the Court, trying without success to regain the influence she

127

had once exerted over Charles. By that time he was staying at La Tremouille's castle at Sully-sur-Loire, where his host encouraged him to indulge his every wish to the full.

Meanwhile the Duke of Burgundy was making the most of his opportunities. The English made him Count of Brie and Count of Champagne, territories that had previously belonged to the crown of France, and paid him 12,500 *livres*. When the English retook Louviers and Soissons, Philippe, in order to reassure his allies, hastened to go to the principal towns which had just been ceded to him, rightly confident that the King of France would make no demur, so completely was he under the influence of his favourites.

Towns which had welcomed Charles before his coronation wrote him urgent letters asking for protection from the English and Burgundians. Getting no reassurance from him they then wrote to Jehanne. She wrote back to Rheims that the Duke of Brittany was sending 3000 men to Charles and hoped they would soon receive good news from him. Finally, probably with her Saints' encouragement, she decided she herself would do what she could to help the threatened towns with or without Charles, believing he would then be bound to support her.

At the beginning of April, carefully avoiding taking leave of him, she quitted Sully. Accompanied by d'Aulon and other loyal friends, she went to Melun where she expected to meet supporters. However, they numbered less than a thousand and were largely made up of Lombardian mercenaries. Of the distinguished captains who had taken part in the Loire campaign only Xaintrailles was there. On April 18th she entered Melun, abruptly evacuated by Jean de Ligny who was holding it for the Duke of Burgundy. While she was there her Saints warned her that the time would come when she would be captured, but when and where they could not say. She decided not to tell her companions, but from that time on she chose to follow their initiative. Riding by Lagny-sur-Marne and Senlis they beat a force of English and Burgundians who tried to bar their way. They arrived on May 13th at Compiegne, which surprisingly enough Regnault de Chartres and the Count of Vendome had reached a few hours previously.

Their presence provided, if indeed it were not designed to

afford, a wonderful opportunity for them to arrange her undoing. The fact that there is no written evidence to support it can hardly shake the generally held belief that she was deliberately betrayed.

One pretext offered for Regnault's unlooked for arrival was to provide for the protection of the city from the Burgundians! Why the Keeper of the Seals should be concerned with military matters is hard to understand. Vendome was known to be very alarmed by Jehanne's political programme. The governor of Compiegne was Guillaume de Flavy, a half-brother of Regnault de Chartres, and a good friend of La Tremouille. Jehanne told her friends in Compiegne that she feared she would be betrayed.

The governor suggested to the captains, in the absence of Jehanne, that they should make a reconnaissance along the Oise to determine the positions occupied by the English and Burgundians. When she heard this plan she said she considered it to have too few advantages to warrant the hazards involved. She was assured that all measures would be taken to facilitate their return to the town – the drawbridge would be kept down, some boats would be available for any latecomers, and the artillery would be ready to fire on the bulwarks beyond the city walls to prevent the enemy reaching the drawbridge. Against her better judgment she left Compiegne.

In spite of her evil presentiments she successfully led a force of five hundred men against an enemy garrison at Margny, and then heard all the bells of Compiegne being rung. As though this was a signal, Jehanne found herself ambushed. Jean de Ligny at the head of a large contingent of Burgundians came down the bank of the river and a body of English soldiers arrived from the opposite direction. Trapped between them she managed to collect her forces and they fought their way back to the walls of Compiegne, only to find that the drawbridge had been raised and there were no boats there. The artillery was silent.

And that was the end of the hopes of la Pucelle, the Third Order, the peasants, the common townspeople, the merchants and the poor clergy for a juster society.

It came out later that as soon as her captors had their hands on her standard they set fire to it and threw the cinders in the river. This was because they were convinced this standard had magical powers on which her victories had depended! Burning and throwing the cinders away would not only protect the people who had handled it, but would also reduce Jehanne's powers in future!

12

Captivity

Captivity

Jehanne was wearing a crimson velvet cape over her armour, and one of the archers of the Bastard de Vendome caught hold of it and pulled her off her horse. She fell flat on her back. As was the normal practice at that time for dealing with important prisoners, she was handed over to Vendome, who in his turn passed her on to his commandant, Jean de Ligny of Luxembourg. It was about six o'clock on May 23rd, 1430. D'Aulon, Pierre Darc, Xaintrailles and others were captured at the same time.

She was rudely handled and insulted as she was taken to the camp at Margny, which had been reoccupied by the Burgundians. The moment the Duke of Burgundy was informed that she had been made a prisoner, he left his fortified residence at Coudon and rushed to see her, taking with him his official historian, Enguerrand de Monstrelet. In Margny they interviewed her, but what was said has never been revealed. Monstrelet who was famous for his good memory could never recall a word that was said! But after this visit Jehanne was treated as a prisoner of rank.

Burgundy of course was fully aware of her parentage, and was desperate that it should be kept a secret. There is no doubt but that he promised she would not be harmed if she kept it undisclosed. It is also equally certain that she refused to promise to lay down her arms should she manage to regain her freedom.

The Valois and the Burgundians shared a common ancestor, the king of France, Jean le Bon. There had been so much intermarrying between them that they were almost like one big family. The elder sister of Philippe, Marguerite, had

131

married the Dauphin Louis, Philippe's first wife had been Michelle, the daughter of Charles VI. Jehanne was a stepsister of Philippe's mother, of Catherine the Queen of England, of Charles of Orleans, and sister (or perhaps Philippe thought stepsister) of the king. To admit Jehanne was the incestuous child of Isabeau would throw a disturbing doubt on the legitimacy of most of them!

At a time when it was not all that unusual to regard assassination as a possible activity for the ambitious thirsting to gain his own ends, one must suppose that the death of Jehanne would have been considered but abandoned, not on moral grounds but because it would be inexpedient, too dangerous, indeed risking irremediable trouble. What might not Isabeau divulge if the Maid were murdered? Isabeau was now bitter, friendless and almost poverty-stricken, bereft of her long paid pension because the English could not forgive her for being the mother of Jehanne. Yolande of Anjou who had succeeded so successfully in making use of Jehanne, could divulge nothing since her daughter was married to the king, but La Hire, Gilles de Rais, Xaintrailles, the courageous bishop of Embrun Jacques Gelu, and the old chancellor of the University of Paris Jean Gerson, wouldn't any or all of them raise their voices if Jehanne were put to death and explain why it had been thought necessary or advisable to kill her?

Philippe was not to know that Jehanne had already sworn an inviolable oath to keep her origin a secret. It is interesting that although he could have demanded that she should be handed over to him, Burgundy was apparently glad to leave her in the hands of Jean de Ligny. He, feeling uncertain that efforts by the French would not be made to free her if she were kept in the castle at Margny, took her to the castle of Beaulieu in Vermandois after a few days. Two weeks later Jehanne nearly escaped. She managed to lock up her guards in the tower where she had been kept, but was spotted by a sentry as she was about to leave. To her great disappointment she was taken back to be locked up again in that same tower where she had been kept before.

But as a result Ligny removed her to his castle of Beaurevoir where his wife Jehanne de Béthune, his daughter-in-law Jehanne de Bar and his aunt Jehanne de Luxembourg, were all living. His aunt was an immensely rich old lady, whose heir

Ligny hoped to be. All three ladies had the best of reasons to hate the English. The first two were the widow and daughter of Robert de Bar who had been killed at Agincourt, and the third was the godmother of Charles VII. And then there were blood ties between them and Jehanne as well. The Duchess of Luxembourg became much attached to Jehanne, so the four months that the Maid spent in this castle were much less traumatic than they might have been. When the possibility of the English paying Ligny the equivalent of a king's ransom for Jehanne arose, his aunt made it clear that she would disinherit him if he accepted it, so he promised not to do so. Her will naming him as her sole heir was signed on September 10th, 1430.

While Jehanne was living at Beaurevoir, Cauchon visited the castle. Whether he was received by the three ladies is not known, but I believe he came primarily to see Jehanne, and warn her that the University of Paris, which was rabidly Dominican, was announcing that she was probably a heretic and witch. Knowing that she was a Franciscan, and a Third Order *Dame très Discrète,* it was out for her blood.

The coronation of Charles at Rheims and his anointing 'by the Grace of God' had taken the English by surprise, and had undermined the status of Henry as king of France. The only way Charles's coronation could be annulled would be if it could be shown that it was really the work of the Devil, and Jehanne was clearly marked out as the Devil's agent. Therefore they averred she should be tried by the Inquisition, and if found guilty burned at the stake. Of course she was a prisoner of war, and as such was entitled to be ransomed, and was in no danger of being killed by her military captors. Gilles de Rais offered Charles the money and so did the Orleanais, but the Inquisition announced that anyone who paid her ransom 'would be committing an intolerable offence against the Divine Majesty' and would therefore also be regarded as a heretic and become liable to find himself before an Inquisitorial court.

In order to protect her, Cauchon had arranged to be appointed her judge on the grounds that she had been captured in his Beauvais diocese. He and the Duke of Bedford would see to it that she did not fall into the hands of the University. I believe he told her this.

Statue of Pierre Cauchon,
Bishop of Beauvais from
his tomb in the Cathedral
of Lisieux.

*(B.N. Coll. Gaignières.
Photo Giraudon)*

It is likely that Cauchon mentioned that Henry was a very nice little boy, and was looking forward to meeting her. Cauchon doubtless would also have made it clear that he himself was fully aware of her real parentage, but that the University was not and it was essential that they should remain in ignorance. He would make it possible for her to be sold – there was no other word for it – to the English king in order to avoid her being taken to Paris. Also, the English would be looking for a scapegoat for their recent defeats, but he could assure her that were she found guilty – and indeed this would probably be necessary – he would guarantee that she would escape execution nevertheless. Presumably he finished by saying this conversation should not be disclosed to anyone else.

Doubtless Jehanne had a lot to discuss with her Saints after this interview, but from what she said later, they believed Cauchon was telling her the truth. And it was inherently likely, for Bedford's wife Anne of Burgundy, was herself a *Dame très Discrète,* and a much loved pupil of Mère Colette, as well as Jehanne's cousin.

I doubt very much if Jehanne had previously had the least idea of what appalling dangers she was running into.

Horrified after her interview with Cauchon to think she would fall into the hands of the English, and having heard that the Burgundians were threatening to kill every child under the age of seven when they took possession of Compiegne which they were besieging, Jehanne made another attempt to escape. She slept in a room on the second floor of a tower built in the outer wall of the castle. In spite of St Catherine telling her not to risk jumping out of the window into the dry ditch at the base of the tower, she asked for the blessing of God and the Virgin, and jumped. She was found lying there the next morning, and did not regain consciousness for a considerable time. Apart from bruises, it seems she was otherwise unhurt, though it was some little time before she fully recovered.

Pierre Cauchon was exceptional in having quite close ties with all the main factions in France at that time. He had been born near Rheims towards the end of the fourteenth century. His father, a bourgeois, had been ennobled. Pierre had been a brilliant student at the University of Paris, and he had been elected rector in 1403. His remarkable competence as a lawyer, his gifts as an orator, and his reputation for advocating reforms, made him widely known in the capital. He was appointed a member of a commission instituted by the young king Charles VI in May 1412 to confiscate the goods of princes of the royal blood who had enriched themselves illegally from the public purse. In 1413 further efforts to reform the institutions of the kingdom were abandoned when the king became mad again. Through no fault of his own Cauchon's reputation suffered as a result of the excesses of the Cabochian riots, and he was no longer welcomed at the Court.

He found himself obliged to accept the help of Jean sans Peur who managed to get him appointed archdeacon of Rheims Cathedral. In 1415 he became the secretary to Isabeau, and was her delegate at the meeting in 1418 which arranged the ill-fated conference designed to settle the civil war at Montereau. His assistant on this occasion was Jean La Tremouille, the brother of Charles's favourite. Cauchon had several meetings at this time with Regnault de Chartres his hierarchical superior, and also with other Armagnac delegates, including Robert de Maçon the dauphin's chancellor, and Gerson, Yolande's fervent supporter. These last two became his lifelong friends.

Cauchon was sent as an observer to the Council of Constance (1414-1418) where his talents as a negotiator were quite outstanding and did much to achieve the unification of a Christendom split for more than half a century into three rival organisations each with its own pope. He was largely responsible for the election of Martin V as acknowledged head of the Roman Catholic Church in Rome. He became Martin's referendary counsellor in 1419 and in the following year in France helped draft the Treaty of Troyes. That year too he was made Bishop of Beauvais, and the Duke of Bedford's chaplain.

The moment the University of Paris learned of Jehanne's capture a letter was sent to the Duke of Burgundy – on May 26th, 1430 – saying politely but firmly that he must deliver to them 'a certain woman named la Pucelle, who was strongly suspected by the Inquisition of many crimes seeming to be heretical'. She was to be handed over to a Dominican monk called Brother Martin who was the Inquisition's represen-tative in France. No mention is made of the Bishop of Beauvais in this letter.

The duke did not reply to this because at that time he was anxious not to appear too pro-English, for he was trying to persuade the pope to be reconciled to the government in London in spite of the fact that it had failed to send him the monies collected by the Bishop of Winchester to fight the heretical Hussites in Bohemia. The English had spent them instead on the war in France. Getting no reply to their letter the University sent two more on July 14th written by the Bishop of Beauvais to the Duke of Burgundy and Jean de

Ligny. 'The Bishop of Beauvais requests the Duke of Burgundy and Monseigneur Jean de Ligny on behalf of His Majesty Henry VI that the woman commonly called Jehanne la Pucelle, prisoner, should be sent to the king in order to deliver her to the Church so that she may be tried as she is suspected of having committed several crimes including sorcery, idolatry, invocation of demons, and many others concerning our faith.' This was followed by an offer that since she was a prisoner of war, a ransom would be paid by the king to those people who might lose by this delivery! The sum of 6000 francs was suggested, but followed by the statement that if this was considered an inadequate sum, since 10,000 francs would be paid for a king or royal personage, the sum offered could be raised to 10,000 francs!

A more blatant travesty of all the canonical and chivalric rules would be hard to imagine, and the rest of Jehanne's trial was really in line with this. I doubt if anyone other than Cauchon could have got away with it, and he certainly ran very real risks, which did in fact cause him considerable difficulties later, and probably prevented his appointment as Bishop of Rouen, a post he had long coveted. But it is certain that if Jehanne had fallen into the hands of the University she would have been tortured without mercy and burned at the stake without delay. After her second attempt at escaping, Philippe ordered her removal to his castle in Arras where she was brought on September 20th by Ligny with a considerable escort of Burgundian soldiers. She was lodged in Bellemotte where the duke generally resided. Here she was treated as a lady of rank though separated from d'Aulon and Pierre Darc. During the six weeks she spent there she received a number of visitors including a priest Jean Naviel who brought her twenty-two gold crowns as a gift from the inhabitants of Tournai – which she was allowed to keep – and she was able to write letters to towns which were supporting Charles VII. She had a long private interview with Jean de Pressy, Burgundy's secretary. It is believed that he informed her of the joint arrangements that had been made by the Courts of Charles and Philippe to make sure that she did not fall into the hands of the University. Saint Catherine told Jehanne she would not be liberated until after she had seen the King of England. After this she made no more attempts to escape.

The old duchess, Jehanne de Luxembourg, feeling that her days were numbered and anxious to be buried in her castle at Crotoy, had been taken there in September. On November 6th her nephew turned up at Bellemotte and the following day he and Jehanne went at once to Crotoy where they arrived on 10th. The old lady, happy to have seen Jehanne again, died on 13th, and Ligny became the very wealthy Duke of Luxembourg.

Cauchon turned up at Crotoy armed with 10,000 francs which he had obtained from Bedford on November 15th. Cauchon had no difficulty in convincing Jean that this was a ransom for Jehanne. Ligny made it clear that the ransom money belonged to the duke of Burgundy, and it was put in the appropriate coffer, before his captive was handed over to the bishop. Wasting no time the University of Paris wrote on November 21st to the king of France and England that they were glad to learn that His Highness had now apprehended the woman known as la Pucelle, at which they felt most joyful, confident that he would order this woman to be brought to justice to atone for the sorcery and scandals that this kingdom had suffered through her.

The letter continued, demanding that the king of France and England should order that she be put immediately in the hands of the Church, that is to say of the reverend father in God their honoured Bishop and Count of Beauvais and the Inquisitorial representative for France. It finished that it would seem most convenient if it were the pleasure of His Highness that the said woman should be brought to this city of Paris for her trial.

The same day they wrote to Cauchon 'We note with extreme astonishment that this woman, commonly called la Pucelle, so long delayed to the prejudice of the faith and ecclesiastical jurisdiction, is actually being put in the hands of the king,' and they continued that if Cauchon had displayed more urgency the woman would have already been tried. They concluded that she should be brought to Paris immediately.

Cauchon had done his best to delay at every turn because he was waiting for the Chapter at Rouen to issue him with *'lettres de territoire'* which were essential if the trial was to take place in Rouen. He was now faced with the problem of preventing any further letters from Paris reaching him. This

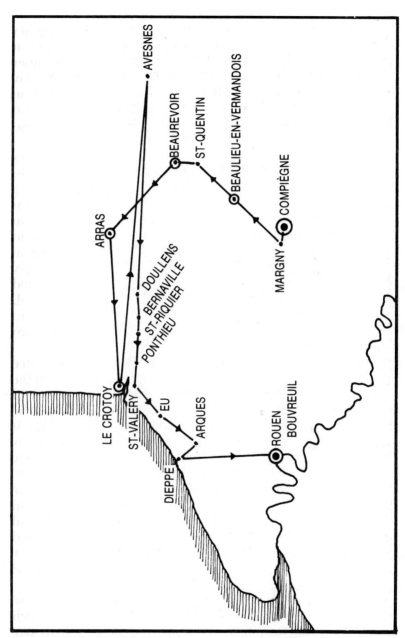

Map showing the castles where Jehanne was imprisoned and the journey
Cauchon made with her from Crotoy to Bouvreuil Castle in Rouen.

explains why in a part of the country which was completely free from any risk of meeting French troops, he led Jehanne from Crotoy to Avesnes, to Doullens, to Bernaville, to Saint-Riquier, to the Ponthieu, to Saint-Valery, to Eu, to Arques and still other places before they went to Rouen!

On December 22nd just before nightfall they reached Rouen, accompanied by a force of fifteen archers. They immediately made for the castle of Bouvreuil where she was to remain until May 30th 1431.

Bouvreuil, built in the thirteenth century, was Bedford's central garrison, his residence, and the sumptuous headquarters of the Royal Family when they were living in France. Any prisoner awaiting trial before an ecclesiastical court should have been detained in one of their own prisons, and there were plenty of them in Rouen. But Jehanne was assigned to a lay building, and at that moment the Queen of England and her son the King were in residence there. Cauchon, on the other hand, lived elsewhere in the city. Jehanne was assigned to an apartment consisting of three rooms, the first of which made use of the whole of the first floor of a tower described as 'opposite the fields'. Some steps led to the other rooms which adjoined the lavish apartments occupied by the Bedfords. Five soldiers were always in the tower room, and four or five jailers were normally in the third room, but they would leave this if Jehanne were receiving visitors or having a meeting with Cauchon and members of the tribunal. There were latrines available, and in the walls were secret hiding places where spies could listen in and from some of them observe what was taking place. Had she been in an ecclesiastical prison she would have been fed on bread and water. Here she enjoyed a normal diet. It is said that the commandant of the jailers, a man called Grilz, was apt to go off to a local tavern, and had to be fetched one time to open the door for two canons of Rouen Cathedral, members of the Tribunal, who wished to interview Jehanne!

Amongst her visitors were Warwick who was the command-ant of Rouen and Bouvreuil, the Duke and Duchess of Bedford, and the Queen Mother of England and her son Henry VI, which encourages one's belief in the reliability of St Catherine's prophecies.

One day a very significant delegation arrived. Jean de

140

Luxembourg turned up accompanied by his brother the Bishop of Therouanne and one of his friends Haimond de Macy. They were taken by Warwick and Stafford to interview the Maid. Ligny is said to have been tormented by his wife for having sold Jehanne to the English in spite of his promise to his aunt, thus besmirching his escutcheon. Macy later related that Luxembourg addressed Jehanne saying to her 'We have come to ransom you, on condition that you will promise not to take up arms against us again.'

Jehanne is said to have replied, 'In the name of God! You are mocking me! You have neither the wish nor the means!'

Ligny repeated his proposal three times, assuring her that he could pay, and she pretended to disbelieve him, and persisted in her refusal in spite of Warwick assuring her that his offer was genuine. I am sure that it was because she did not feel justified in gaining her liberty by making such a promise, and could not explain to these people that her Saints still pressed her to complete her mission. She quite simply could not promise to stop fighting them. Macy then explained that he had come because he had fallen in love with her when he had seen her in the castle of Beaulieu, and he had obtained the permission of Charles VII to marry her and her ransom would be paid if she accepted him. She refused him too, and the delegation left empty handed.

Those essential *'lettres de territoire'* for which Cauchon was waiting, gave a bishop the right of jurisdiction in a diocese other than his own. They were not forthcoming because the canons of Rouen Cathedral were afraid it would lead to Cauchon becoming the incumbent of their vacant diocese, and he was the last person they wanted. It was only because of pressure from Bedford that at last they did provide the papers on December 28th 1430.

Cauchon believed that the larger the Tribunal trying Jehanne the easier it would be for him to control it, so he appointed an unprecedented number of assessors, no fewer than ninety-five religious authorities and theologians. It included Dominicans, White Friars, Franciscans, Benedictines, Augustines, twenty canons, ten superiors of monasteries and six bishops. He nominated his vicar-general d'Estivet, his usher the dean of the Chapter Jean Massier, and the notaries

141

Manchon and Collés, so all the machinery, as it were. was in his hands. But what could he do about the representative of the Inquisition in France? Brother Jean Graverand in matters of the faith was the supreme competent judge. The Bishop of Beauvais said that in spite of anything he had been able to do or say, the Inquisitor would not turn up at the opening ceremony, but took himself off to Constance. As a result everything came to a halt for two months. The authorities were quite unable to explain Graverand's attitude, and there was a general tendency for the assessors to melt away.

The Pope was the sole person in control of the Inquisition. Cauchon's confidential post as his Referendary Councillor now proved invaluable. The Pope wished to discuss with Cauchon all the implications of this trial before giving instructions to his representative, and it was because Graverand had had no papal advice on the subject, that he, with Cauchon's connivance, had taken himself off to Switzerland. Graverand made no complaint about Jehanne being in Bouvreuil instead of an ecclesiastical prison at any time. Had he stayed in Rouen it is very doubtful if he could have avoided doing so, and she could not have continued to live where she did. Even Jean le Maître, an inquisitorial official who had been associated with the early moves on the part of the University, was absent from the first sitting of the Tribunal, which was held on January 9th, 1431.

On February 22nd Cauchon wrote a letter to Graverand saying, 'Since this affair particularly concerns your office of Inquisitor, for it requires you to clarify the causes of heresy, we summon and require your venerable Fatherhood to return at once to this city so that you may perform your office.'

Once again Cauchon overstepped his rights since he had no authority to summon and require the representative of the Inquisition to do anything. Graverand took no offence however, and was prepared to give his local representative Le Maître instructions to be present at the trial but with no right to comment! The inquisitor's deputy was in no hurry to attend, and turned up for the first time on March 13th.

13

The papacy, fully aware that it was unthinkable that a royal princess should be tortured and burned at the stake, was careful to avoid being responsible for Jehanne's trial. Moreover the way Cauchon bent all the rules meant that any judgment it might come to was almost asking to be quashed. It is not true, however, that Jehanne was denied any advocates. More than once she was offered them, but turned them down as she preferred to rely on her heavenly Counsellors. But it is true that she was denied the right of appealing to the Pope. Cauchon gave the Inquisition the opportunity to assert its sole responsibility, but since it did not care to take it, it allowed him to manage the trial as he saw fit. Later the Inquisition rightly claimed it had had nothing to do with it, from beginning to end.

Meanwhile Cauchon was carefully confiscating any evidence that was favourable to Jehanne, for instance a report by Master Nicholas Bailli, a royal notary from Andelot, who had been put in charge of enquiries about her in Lorraine and the Barrois. (Years later Bailli complained bitterly that Cauchon had never paid him for the work he had put in on this, and never used the report either!) And Cauchon set out to terrify anyone offering Jehanne sound advice or undermining in some way his plan to keep the University convinced that she was going to be found guilty.

By and large the attitude that the Maid exhibited during the trial can only reinforce the conviction that she did believe Cauchon was really aiming to save her from execution, even though there was one time when she was sure he had betrayed her. The extraordinary journey from Crotoy to Rouen must have afforded them an unrivalled opportunity to get to know each other, and for him to be able to explain his tactics to some extent and warn her what to expect. But she would not have been able to talk about her revelations – though during the trial she did get her Saints' permission to reveal quite a lot of information about them. More important, however, her Saints assured her that she was going to escape, though how and when was never revealed to her. Much of the time during the trial she behaved as though she were a haughty ruler being arraigned by rebellious subjects; sometimes she showed how sharp her intelligence was; and at others she was simply reduced to tears. Cauchon's behaviour too was just as unpredictable, sometimes sympathetic and understanding, at others authoritarian, whether insisting on sticking to the rules or blatantly ignoring them. But the conduct of both is utterly incomprehensible unless one supposes there was an underlying understanding between them.

The first public sitting of the court took place on February 21st 1431 in the chapel royal in the castle at Rouen. Cauchon opened the proceedings by explaining that this girl Jehanne was accused of many crimes against orthodoxy, and they were assembled here to investigate matters of faith. He then demanded that Jehanne with her hand on a missal should swear to speak the truth, to which she immediately replied that not knowing what questions she would be asked she could make no such promise, as there were some things she had sworn to keep secret and she would be unable to talk about them. After some argument she said that God had revealed some things to her that only Charles was to be told, and she would refuse to answer questions about them, adding a moment later that within a week she would know if she could reveal some of them. Then she said that she was quite ready to tell the truth about information dealing with her mother and father, things that had happened since she came to France, and matters concerning her faith. On this basis her oath was accepted.

Asked her name and address she answered that at home she was called Jeanette and in France Jehanne, but she did not know her surname. Asked where she was born she answered Domremy which was joined to Greux, and Greux had the larger church. Asked the names of her parents she said

144

Sketch of Jehanne with her standard, drawn on a page of the record of her trial in Rouen.

Jacques Darc and Isabelle, and later informed the court of the names of several of her numerous godparents and the name of the pastor who had christened her in Domremy. She told them that her age was 'about nineteen'. Presumably she was fully aware of the Catholic doctrine of *'the right of mental restriction'* which gave her not merely the right to tell lies, but was indeed, in certain circumstances, her duty to do so. One wonders if this was one of the subjects she and Cauchon had discussed during their travels together. Such lies had to be recalled in one's next confession to be absolved.

She was asked to say the Paternoster but said she could only say it after confession. She said much later that it was because she was anxious to confess that she took this line, but it never produced the right result for her. On the contrary, because it was believed generally that witches always made a mistake when saying it, that her refusal counted against her.

Told that she was forbidden to leave the castle, she answered so as to make it clear to the Tribunal that if she were able to escape no one would be able to say that she had violated any promises, as she had never given any such undertaking and every prisoner had the right to escape if he could.

The following day there was a similar argument about swearing to tell the truth, settled in the same way. This pantomime happened every time the court met.

Asked a variety of questions including once more what her age was, she answered that she did not know. She told them her mother had taught her her prayers, she had learned to sew and spin, looked after household affairs when at home, and never looked after her father's sheep or other animals. Normally she confessed to the vicar, but if he were not free, with his permission she confessed to someone else. Two or three times she had confessed to some Mendicant Friar. At Easter she received Holy Communion.

Then she told them that 'When I was thirteen years old I heard a voice coming from God to help me control myself. The first time I was very frightened. It happened at midday, it was summertime. In my father's garden. You should know I had not been fasting, nor had I fasted the day before. I heard a voice to my right, by the side of the church. Nearly always there is a radiance which comes with it. This light is on the same side as the voice. It is a bright light. When I was in France I heard the voice very often. That first time the light was there.

'If I was in a wood I would hear the voice clearly coming towards me. It was lovely to hear. I believe it was sent by God. When I had heard it for the third time I believed it was the voice of an angel. The voice has always protected me. And I have always understood it.

It has helped me to behave as I should, to go frequently to church, it told me what it was necessary for me to know, and said that I must go to France . . . But for today I'm not going to tell you in what form the voice has appeared to me . . . Two or three times a week my voice told me I must go to France to raise the siege of Orleans but I said I was a poor girl who knew nothing about war or horses. The voice told me I must not stay where I was but I must find Robert de Baudricourt in Vaucouleurs – he was the captain at that place – and that he would find people who would come with me. My voice said I mustn't let my father know that I was leaving. So then I went to my uncle's home. I wanted to stay there for a while. I stayed about a week. I told my uncle he should take me to Vaucouleurs, and my uncle took me there.

When I arrived at Vaucouleurs I recognised Robert de Baudricourt though I had never seen him before. It was the voice which told me who he was. I told him I had to go to France. Twice he refused me but the third time he gave me some people. The voice had told me this would happen. I knew nothing of fighting or riding.

The Duke of Lorraine asked that I should be taken to him. I went and I told him that I ought to go to France. He asked me if he would get better – he was ill – I told him I didn't know anything about things like that. I talked to him a little about my going to France and asked him to let his son and other people take me to France, and I would pray for his health. I had gone with a safe-conduit and came back the same way to Vaucouleurs. After I'd left Vaucouleurs I reached Saint-Urbain and I slept at the abbey. I was wearing men's clothes. Baudricourt had given me a sword. I hadn't any other arms. An equerry and four soldiers came with me. On the way I passed through Auxerre. I heard mass in the cathedral. I often heard my voices on the journey.

Robert de Baudricourt had made the men swear that they would take me there safely. He said to me, "Well now I'm taking leave of you. Go! And come what may." '

During this long account she was interrupted now and again, but never attempted to answer the questions she was asked, brushing them aside with an impatient *'Passez outre!'* which would seem almost as though she had said 'Don't interrupt!' and went on with her recital regardless. But perhaps because she stopped for breath at this juncture or there was a combined assault, she did then give the following answers to questions:

I know that God loves the Duke of Orleans. I have had more revelations about him than any other living person except the king.'

'It was really necessary for me to have men's clothing. I believe that my Counsel was right to advise me to.'

'I sent a letter to the English who were besieging Orleans telling them to stop fighting. I have seen a copy of it since I came to Rouen.'

147

She then continued, 'I had no difficulty in seeing the king. In Sainte-Catherine de Fierbois I sent a letter to the king at Chinon. I arrived about midday and stayed at an inn. After lunch I went to the king's castle I recognized him amongst the others by what my voices had told me. I told the king I wanted to lead the war against the English.'

'When your voices described the king, was there that light in that place?' Master Beaupère asked.

'*Passez outre!*' she replied.

'Did you by chance see an angel above your king?' he persisted.

'Leave me alone! *Passez outre*. Before the king had me to help him he himself had many apparitions and lovely revelations.'

'What apparitions? What revelations?' Beaupère asked.

'I shall not tell you. Go and ask the king, he will tell you.'

'The voice had promised me that the king would receive me as soon as I arrived. The people in my party knew very well that the voice had been sent by God, it is possible to see the voice and recognize it. I know it, I'm certain of it. The King, and many other people with him can hear and see the voice that comes to me. Charles de Bourbon was there and two or three others.

'There isn't a single day when I don't hear the voice, and I do need it. I have never asked anything of it for myself, except the wellbeing of my soul. It was my voice which told them to stay at Saint Denis in France. And I wanted to stay there, but I was forced to leave by people more powerful than myself. Had I not been wounded I wouldn't have left Saint-Denis. However in five days I was better, and I had a skirmish then against Paris.'

'Wasn't that on a Sunday?' he asked.

'I think it may have been,' she answered.

'Was it right for you to fight on a Sunday?'

'*Passez outre!*'

In the hope that they would be able to prove that Jehanne was a witch, she was obliged once more to undergo a physical examination to demonstrate that she was in fact a virgin. This time it was the Duchess of Bedford who was asked with other highborn ladies to undertake the task. It is said that it was so arranged that the Duke was able to make use of a conveniently placed spyhole so that he was able to corroborate that she was in fact an undoubted virgin.

At the third public session there was a long series of questions about her 'voice'. She said that it had woken her up that morning, that she did not know if it was in her room or not, but certainly it was in the castle, and it had told her to answer boldly any questions she was asked. Yes, the light was there when she heard the voice, she often heard it three times a day, and the light would appear each time.

She saw fit, too, to warn Cauchon that because she had received her mission from God, he was putting himself in some danger by frustrating her from carrying out what He had ordered her to do.

Later they began asking her about her childhood, did she know anything about a very old, large tree? Yes, an ash tree. It was near Domremy, it was called the Ladies' Tree or Fairies' Tree. There was a day during the summer when the children took flowers and decorated it, and had a picnic there, and sang songs to it. There was a spring nearby which was supposed to have curative properties, but Jehanne had no idea whether it had or not. No, she had never seen fairies there – nor elsewhere – some old people in the village said they had; one of them was one of her godmothers, but she had no idea if she had been telling the truth. Another time she was asked about mandragore. She said she had never had any, or even seen any and did not know what properties it was supposed to have. She had heard it was supposed to be found underground, perhaps near the Fairies' Tree.

She was asked if the voice ever contradicted itself, and she denied it had ever happened. Then she was asked if it had forbidden her to answer some of their questions, and she refused to answer that very one, and some others. Then she said, 'Give me those questions in writing.' Asked again if she had ever helped with her father's animals she said that on an occasion when the village had been threatened by soldiers she had helped drive them into the safety of the castle grounds.

Towards the end of the session she was asked if she knew anything about a wood called the Bois Chenu. One could see it she said from the threshold of her father's house, about a mile and a half away. She had never heard that it was where fairies were seen, but her brother had told her that people said she had accepted a proposal of marriage there. But she told him, the fact was quite the contrary. And soon after she had met the king he asked her if she had heard that people were saying that according to some prophets a girl was living there who could perform miracles. 'I said I didn't believe it.'

Then she was asked if she would wear women's clothes. She answered, 'When it pleases God that I should.'

On the following day, the fourth audience, on Tuesday February 27th, Jehanne was asked if the voices had forbidden her to reveal their revelations without their permission. She answered she wished they would get a copy of the *Livres de Poitiers* as she had answered then if God wished it. Asked in what form St Michael had appeared she said she hadn't permission to say.

Had there been an angel over the king's head the first time she saw him? If there were one she had not seen him. One feels she was getting tired of these questions, and when asked, 'Was there a light on the king's head?' she replied, 'Yes I think so. There were three hundred courtiers there and fifty torches without counting any spiritual light.'

Then she revealed that she had had permission to describe her 'voice' in much more detail. There were in fact two voices, and they were the voices of Saint Catherine and Saint Margaret. Of course she could distinguish one from the other! She had known them for seven years! They had told her their names themselves. It was always these saints who gave her advice, and she always took it, because she felt if she did not, they would stop coming to see her.

Asked which saint came to her first, she replied it was St Michael. 'I saw him in front of my eyes. He was not alone but accompanied by angels from Heaven. I saw them just as I am seeing you. When they left I wept, because I wanted them to take me with them.'

They kept on asking her, again and again, if she saw this light and she repeated that almost invariably, if there were a voice there was a light too.

They asked how the king had come to believe that her revelations came from God. She said it was because he believed a sign she had given him, it had been revealed to her to tell him only, and nothing would make her tell anyone else.

Then they asked her about the sword from Fierbois, and suggested she had said prayers over it to make it lucky.

'No.'

Or perhaps she had left it on an altar?

'No.'

She said she had offered a sword and armour to Saint Denis, but it was not this sword. Nor was it the sword she was using when she was taken prisoner, that one had been taken from a Burgundian. She believed her brother was looking after the one from Fierbois.

Her standard was then the subject of questions. The Third Order was not mentioned, but she was asked whether she preferred it or her sword?

She said she loved the standard forty times more than the sword. She always carried her standard when she went into battle, so that she shouldn't kill people. 'I have never killed anyone,' she added.

Yes, she had known through her saints in advance that she would be wounded, she had said so to the king. But her saints had helped her, and she had been able to return to the fighting the same day. The wound healed in a fortnight.

Why hadn't she concluded a truce with the captain at Jargeau? Because they had asked for a fortnight's truce. She had offered them instead a safe conduct with their horses and arms if they liked to leave in small parties during the next hour. Otherwise they could expect an assault. They had chosen to leave.

Asked if she had discussed this ultimatum with her saints she answered, 'I don't remember.'

At the fifth audience on March 1st, after taking the usual oath on the New Testament, she volunteered that she would speak the truth as though she was in front of the Pope of Rome about anything touching the trial, which elicited the inquiry if she believed he was the true pope? Jehanne asked if there were two? After some discussion she averred that she believed in the Pope in Rome.

She was then asked if she was in the habit when writing letters to include the names Jhesus-Maria with a cross?

'It depends. Sometimes I put a cross in order to tell the

151

person I'm writing to, that he doesn't have to do what I've said in the letter.'

They then read out at length a letter that she had written to the King of England and the Duke of Bedford. Had she written this, they asked?

'Very nearly. You say "Give back to the Maid," whereas I wrote "Give back to the King." And you say "Head of the army" and "body for body". I mentioned neither. No head of the army dictated that letter, I dictated it. And I say that before seven years have passed the English will suffer a defeat much greater than that of Orleans, and they will lose the whole of France . . . It will be a great victory that God will send the French.'

Asked how she knew this she said by revelation, but she did not know the day or the hour. She knew it because Saint Catherine and Saint Margaret had told her, yesterday and today. She was asked if they always wore the same clothes, and she answered they always wore most beautiful crowns, 'But I don't know what dresses they have.'

Asked how she knew whether they were men or women, she answered, 'By their voices. And I know that what they say is by the commandment of God.'

'What kind of form do you see?' she was asked, and answered:

'Their faces.'

'Have they got hair?'

'What a funny question!'

'Is there anything between the hair and the crown. Is the hair long and hanging down?'

'I don't know at all. I don't know if they have arms or other limbs. They speak very well, and elegantly, and I understand them easily.'

'How are they able to speak if they have no limbs?'

'I'll ask God. Their voices are beautiful, soft and gentle, and they speak French.'

'Doesn't Saint Margaret speak English?'

'Why should she speak English when she doesn't support the English side?'

'On their heads, besides their crowns do they wear gold rings or anything?'

'I've no idea.'

Later in this session they asked about St Michael; what he looked like, when she had last seen him, did he have hair, did he have his balance with him? Was he naked? To which Jehanne responded with 'Do you suppose God has nothing to dress him in?'

She said she hadn't seen him wearing a crown, or carrying a balance, she knew nothing about what clothes he wore, she didn't know whether he had hair or not, she last saw him in the castle at Crotoy. But she added spontaneously that to see him was a great joy to her, he gave her great comfort. It seemed to her that when she saw him she was sure she was not in a state of mortal sin.

Then her judges tried once more to make her tell them about 'The Sign' she had given the king so that he should believe she was inspired by God. Once more she said she would simply perjure herself if she told them.

'I have always told you that you will not drag this from my lips. I will not tell you what concerns my king.'

They asked to whom she had made these promises and she said to Saint Catherine and Saint Margaret. And she had done this because so many people tried to make her tell them.

They asked if she was alone with the king when she told him, and she said yes, but there were a lot of people around.

'When you told him, did you see a crown on his head?'

'I cannot reply without perjuring myself.'

'When your king was in Rheims had he a crown?'

'On my advice he was pleased to use the crown that was already there. But another, much more precious, was brought to him later. At the request of the people in Rheims he was asked to keep their crown as then they did not have to pay soldiers to guard it! But since then the king has a crown which is a thousand times more valuable.'

'Have you seen this very precious crown?'

'I cannot tell you without breaking my promise. If I haven't seen it, I have heard how valuable it is.'

The sixth audience was heard on Saturday March 3rd. After the usual sparring about oaths and what constituted the proper subject to be discussed as relevant to the trial, her judge wanted to know if the king had demanded when he first saw her if she had had a revelation telling her to wear men's clothes.

'I don't remember. But it will be recorded in the report from Poitiers.'

'Was the question of your change of clothing discussed in Poitiers and Chinon?'

'I don't remember. If they asked me when it happened I would have told them it was in Vaucouleurs.'

'And your king, and the queen, and people generally, did none of them suggest you should abandon men's clothes?'

'That is no part of your trial!'

'At the Beaurevoir castle, had no one questioned it?'

'Yes, they did. I told them I would not change without an order from God. Mlle de Luxembourg and Mme de Beaurevoir offered me a woman's dress or cloth to make one, and asked me to wear it. But I answered that I had not leave to do so. The time to change had not yet arrived.'

She went on to explain that other people, except her Queen, (meaning Yolande) had behaved in the same way.

'When you started working for the king and had your banner made did the gentlemen in the army tend to copy it for themselves?' she was asked.

'The gentlemen all tended to keep their own coats of arms, except for a few friends who were in my particular small company – I only had two or three lances. They did tend to copy it to some extent, but it was really so that they could be recognized as being my men.'

'Were the banners often renewed?'

'I don't know. When they got broken they were replaced.'

'Were they regarded as lucky?'

'I used to say to my people, "Go boldly among the English!" and I went there myself with them. I just told them what had happened before and it happened again.'

And so the questioning went on, suggesting that the white satin made into banners had been wrapped around altars before being cut up, that Jhesus-Maria was written on them, and that they had been sprinkled with holy water. She denied having indulged in any such practices. Then they asked what was the round thing that she had worn on the back of her helmet when she was attacking Jargeau.

'But there wasn't anything there!'

154

They inquired about her participation in christenings of babies in various towns that she had visited, and she agreed if the naming were left to her she called the little boys Charles, after the king, and the little girls Jehanne. In Lagny she was told when she arrived that all the girls in the place were on their knees in front of Notre Dame, praying that a three day old baby should be restored to life, and she went there and joined them. The baby looked quite black, but after a time it yawned and its colour changed and for a short while it became alive and it was christened, but then it turned black again and was buried in consecrated ground. She agreed that at many of the places many women came up to her and touched her hands and her rings, but she didn't understand why they were doing it.

And what, she was asked, had taken place the first time she met Brother Richard?

'As he approached me he was crossing himself and sprinkling holy water around, and I said to him, 'Don't be afraid, I shan't fly away!' She couldn't remember if he had returned to Troyes with them or not.

'Didn't he preach a sermon about you?'

'I don't know anything about any sermon. I wasn't there long, I didn't sleep there.'

'Did you see Catherine de la Rochelle?' (She was a visionary La Tremouille had given publicity to, in the hope of devaluing Jehanne's status).

'Yes, in Jargeau and Montfaucon in Berry.'

'Did she show you a white lady who she said visited her?'

'No.'

'What did she say?'

'She said the white lady would enable the king to find hidden treasure and that it would be handed over to him, and he could pay my army with it. I told her to go home and look after her husband and family. Saint Catherine and Saint Margaret told me she was a fraud. I went to bed with her one night but I fell asleep, and in the morning I asked if the lady had come, and she said she had, but they could not wake me up. So I slept during the next day, and stayed awake all night, but she still didn't appear. When I kept asking if she was going to turn up, I was told 'Yes! Yes! Very soon,' but she didn't

155

come. So I wrote to the king and told him not to bother with her. Brother Richard and Catherine were very annoyed with me.'

Jehanne mentioned that her voices had told her after Melun had fallen into their hands, that the time would come when she would be captured, but she was not told when. She did not tell anyone else. But after it had happened, and she had tried unsuccessfully to escape, she was assured that she would be freed but not until she had seen the King of England.

On March 3rd, while denying that it was part of her trial, she admitted that she did not know either the day or the hour when she would escape.

'Have your voices made any general remarks about it?' she was asked and she replied: 'Yes, indeed, they have said that I would be delivered, but I know neither the day nor the hour. They also said that I should show a cheerful face.'

On March 17th she said she firmly believed that . . . God would soon save her, and by a miracle. On March 18th Saint Catherine had assured her she would be rescued.

'I don't know if I shall be taken from the prison, or during the trial, or because of some trouble or other, but I think it will be one or the other. I staunchly believe in what my voices have told me: that I shall be saved!'

And so the questioning went on, in a singularly haphazard way. At the end of the session, which was the last of the planned 'preliminary audiences', Cauchon announced that each of the members of the Tribunal would be given a transcript of the proceedings up to the present and when they had studied this they would discuss their findings, and a list would be drawn up of those matters which they wished to investigate further. Master Jean de la Fontaine would conduct the Complementary Interrogations that would then have become necessary.

14

Complementary Interrogations

Everything that was said at these audiences was supposed to be written down, and at the end of the day the two notaries made as accurate a record of the proceedings as they were able, and having signed it gave it to Cauchon. The proceedings of course were normally all held in French, and the notaries delivered their version in French. But Cauchon retained the documents instead of sending them to Paris as the University pressed him to do, insisting that they should first be translated into Latin, a task he undertook to oversee himself! The translation was carried out by Thomas de Courcelles and Guillaume Manchon. It was an incredible six years before he delivered the document. The original French version has not survived except for some parts, and the accuracy of the Latin version is at times suspect, where it is possible to compare the two. There was, however, another 'secret' version made by another scribe privately engaged by Cauchon, who sat behind a curtain writing down an accurate record including matters 'off the record'. This came to light after Cauchon's death.

There is a passage in the Third Interrogation which I find highly significant, but generally it seems to be regarded by the authors I have read, as a rather unexpected example of Jehanne being prepared to lead the Tribunal up the garden path. In previous sessions she had been pressed over and over again to explain the nature of the 'Sign' she had given to the dauphin which convinced him that her revelations really came from God. She protested that nothing would make her reveal it. I believe that Cauchon assumed it was her real parentage that she was talking about, and he was quite unaware that she had told Charles another even more important secret about the priory of Sion.

Jehanne, perhaps inadvertently, misled her questioners in telescoping that secret she told Charles in the embrasure in Chinon, and 'the sign' which was manifested in her Poitiers' hallucination. She quite honestly believed that that had been experienced by Charles and the archbishop and various courtiers she believed were close to him when the angel gave him the crown as a 'sign', and she believed too that the rest of the courtiers had seen the crown itself, but had not seen the angel.

She was convinced the crown had been put safely away in the king's treasury and could have been fetched for the coronation, had there been time.

In the First Complementary Interrogation Master Jean de la Fontaine asked, 'What is the sign which came to your king?'

When she answered, 'It is beautiful and honourable, good to believe and the most precious thing you can imagine.'

I think she may well have been momentarily thinking of the sacred blood which ran in his wife's veins.

'But this sign, does it still continue in being?'

'Assuredly, it will last a thousand years, and more! It is part of the king's treasure.'

Did she at this moment realize she was possibly taking a risk of revealing something that must be kept hidden? If so, she would have felt relieved when his next question was: 'Is it gold? . . . Silver? . . . A precious stone? . . . A crown?'

'I shan't tell you anything else; one does not know how to describe anything that is as valuable as the sign. It was an angel who for the sake of God and someone else, brought the sign to the king, and I thank Our Lord for it.'

'Did any churchmen see the sign?'

'When the king and those who were with him saw the sign, and even the angel who brought it, I asked the king if he were content, and he replied that he was. Then I left and went into a little chapel, quite close; afterwards I heard them say when I had gone, more than three hundred people had seen the sign. It was for love of me and to stop people asking me questions, that God had allowed the people who support me to see the sign.'

158

'And did you and the king not make a reverence to the angel who brought it?'

'Yes, I did. I knelt and took off my hat.'

At the Third Complementary Interrogation the following questions and answers took place. I have kept the order unchanged.

'The sign, brought to your king, what was it?'

'The angel brought him a crown and confirmed that with the aid of God and by means of my labour, he would rule over the whole kingdom of France, so he should set to work to provide me with men at arms, Otherwise he would not be crowned or anointed for a long time.'

'In what way did the angel bring the crown? Did he put it on your king's head?'

'It was given to an archbishop, that of Rheims it seemed to me, in the presence of the king; the archbishop received it and offered it to the king.'

'Where was it brought to?'

'To the king's room in the castle at Chinon.'

'What day? What time?'

'The day, I don't know. The time? The sun was high. I really don't remember. It was the month of April or March, it will be two years ago next April, or this month. After Easter.'

'The first day that you saw the sign, did the king see it too?'

'Yes, he had it himself.'

'What was this crown made of?'

'Of fine gold, of course! And so rich I don't know how to describe it. The crown signified that the king would possess the kingdom of France.'

'Did it have any precious stones?'

'I have said all I know about it.'

'Did you touch or kiss it?'

'No.'

'The angel who brought it, did he come from on high or on the ground?'

'He came from on high. I mean he came because Our Lord ordered it. He entered through the door of the room.'

'He came forward on the ground after he had entered the room?'

'When he arrived in front of the king he made a bow, and

leaning towards him said what I have told you the crown meant; and then he praised the patience the king had shown in the great tribulations he had suffered.'

'How far was the threshold from the king?'

'I should say about as long as a lance. The angel went back the way he had come.'

'When the angel came I accompanied him, I went with him up the staircase to the king's room. The angel went in first, and I said to the king 'Sire, here is your sign. Take it!'

'Where were you when the angel appeared to you?'

'I spent most of my time praying that God would send the king a sign. I was in my lodging, the home of a good woman who lived near the Chinon castle when he came. Then we went together to where the king lived. He was accompanied by a number of other angels, but nobody saw them.

'I think it was for love of me and to rid me of anxiety caused by people pestering me, that a number of people passing us did not see the angels.'

'All the people who were with the king saw the angel?'

'I think that the Archbishop of Rheims, the Lords d'Alençon, La Tremouille, and Charles de Bourbon saw him. As for the crown, many churchmen and other people saw it who did not see the angel.'

'What did he look like? How big was he?'

'I am not allowed to tell you. I'll answer that tomorrow.'

'Did the angels accompanying him all look like him?'

'Some of them resembled him, others not, as far as I could see. Some had wings, some had crowns. Saint Margaret and Saint Catherine were there, and other saints as well, all in the king's room.'

'How did the angel leave you?'

'In the little chapel. I was really dismayed at his going. I should so much have liked to go with him! I mean to say: my soul.'

'When he went did you stay joyful or much afraid, terrified?'

'He didn't leave me afraid or terrified. But I was disappointed when he left.'

'Do you think you warranted God sending you an angel?'

'He came for something important in the hope that the king

would believe in the sign and that people would stop worrying me. It was to give help to the good people in Orleans, and increase the reputation of the king and the good Duke of Orleans.'

'But why you rather than someone else?'

'It pleased God that a simple girl would be able to drive back the king's adversaries.'

'Were you told where the angel had got the crown?'

'He had brought it from God. There is no goldsmith in the world who could have fashioned it so beautifully and so intricately. I will ask God where he got it. I shan't know otherwise where it came from.'

'This crown, did it smell good? Had it a pleasant odour? Was it at all sparkling?'

'I don't remember – I'll try . . . Yes, it did smell good. But it will be well guarded because it is so becoming! Yes, it is a special sort of crown.'

'Has the angel written any letters?'

'No.'

'What evidence did the king and the people with him and you yourself have, that it really was an angel?'

'The king believed it because of the teaching of the churchmen who were there, and by the sign of the crown.'

'But how did these churchmen know that they could believe it was an angel?'

'By their learning and because they were clerics.'

It is clear to me that Jehanne was here describing the hallucination which occurred in Poitiers about the same time that the two monks brought back the report 'from Domremy and Vaucouleurs', which resulted in the Commissioners' endorsement of Jehanne's bona fides. The cessation of the interminable questioning she had had to put up with, followed by the Court going to Tours with its encouraging activities there, would have convinced her that Charles had clearly been influenced by the visit of the angel. It would seem to me quite out of character for her to have made up the whole episode anyway. I believe too the fact that she agreed that the crown had a pleasant smell, also points to her having suffered a hallucination. But this episode in her trial is very awkward to explain for those many authors who do not believe in the reality of her visions.

After these interrogations the 'wise men' assembled in Cauchon's residence on March 18th and took away their papers to analyse Jehanne's answers to their questions and consider the real meaning of her refusal to undertake to speak the truth on all subjects. On Saturday March 24th Cauchon announced that having examined the Interrogatories, and found that thanks to the Grace of God they would contribute to the exaltation of the Faith, he had decided that he and some members of the Tribunal should visit Jehanne in her prison and Guillaume Manchon would read to the accused a summary of the proceedings to date and get her to swear that she would not add any untruths to the answers she had already given.

During this lecture the only comment she made was to say that her surname was either Darc or Romée, and that in her country girls usually took the surname of their mothers. She then asked that all the questions and answers she had given should be read out to her. This was done. She made no alterations.

On Sunday March 25th another small party of men went with Cauchon to visit her and exhorted her to wear women's clothes, in reward for which she would be allowed to attend mass on Easter Sunday and take Communion. She said that if they would provide her with a long woman's dress, without a train, she would put it on and gladly go to mass. Questions elicited however that she intended to keep her men's clothes on underneath, and so she was denied the opportunity of going to church.

After all these preliminary activities, the trial proper took place on the 26th, 27th and 28th of March in Cauchon's residence. The first day the Tribunal confirmed that she should be accused and then what actual words were to be used in the Articles of the Act of Accusation. It contained sixty-six counts! Each of the assessors deliberated over the actual procedure to be adopted. On March 27th the President offered the accused, 'because she was not sufficiently learned or instructed in such difficult matters, some eminent ecclesiastics, experts in divine and human law who would help her with pity and forbearance.'

Jehanne thanked them all for their solicitude for her wellbeing and also for their offer of help, but explained that she had no intention of abandoning the counsel of God.

Finally on Wednesday March 28th the articles of the Act of Accusation were read out to her. Briefly it averred that:

The woman Jehanne, commonly known as The Maid, was charged with being a sorceress, devious guesser, pseudo-prophetess, invocatress of evil and conspiring spirits, superstitious, given to magical arts, thinking ill of the catholic faith, schismatic of the article *Unam Sanctam,* corrupted, sacrilegious, idolatrous, apostate, slanderous and malignant, a blasphemer of God and his saints, scandalous and seditious disturber of the peace, an alien to peace, an advocate of war, cruelly thirsting for human blood, and implacable for its spilling, so lacking in shame as to deny all the decency of her sex, to dress irreverently in unwonted clothes, and adopt the stance of a man of war, abominable for so many transgressions against God and man, a betrayer of trust in divine and natural law such as ecclesiastical discipline, a seducer of princes and people, accepting the kissing of her hands and clothes in defiance of God whom one venerates and adores, a usurper of honours and divine worship, a heretic (or at least strongly suspected of heresy), and she should, for all these transgressions, be canonically and legally chastised.

163

15

Trial and Abjuration

While Jehanne was waiting for further developments Cauchon sent her a stuffed pike for her dinner. She suffered from food poisoning as a result and needed medical attention. She was bled. In spite of which she survived.

Her next official meeting took place in her apartment on April 18th. Cauchon said the doctors and lawyers had come to her wishing for her speedy restoration to health. He continued at considerable length to explain that as she was illiterate and did not know how to write, they had come to offer her whatever help might be necessary to bring her to understand the dangerous situation she found herself in.

Jehanne replied that seeing how ill she was, she considered that she was in great danger of dying, and that in these circumstances she would like to confess and be promised Christian burial. This would be granted her, she was told, if she submitted to the Church. To which she replied and I think she meant it as a warning, if not a threat, that if she died in prison and was not buried properly, she would tell Our Lord about it.

Cauchon then asked her, 'Don't you imagine that God could give some revelations about you to someone who was quite unknown to you?'

'Yes, of course!' she replied. 'But whatever happens to me I shall not say anything different to what I've said during the trial.' And after a good deal more equally fruitless discussion, she concluded, 'I hope that the Church and Catholics will pray for me.'

On May 2nd the whole Tribunal met in a room in the castle near the great hall. Jehanne was also there. The meeting had been called so that a famous learned and venerable professor of Theology, Master Jean de Chatillon, Archdeacon of Evreux, could join in their exhortations for her to see the error of her ways, and be willing to submit to the Church Militant. He went through the entire proceedings at length, and at the end Jehanne said that she had not changed her mind.

At long last he asked, 'Would you submit to Our Holy Father the Pope?'

'Take me to him and I will answer him,' she replied.

'And on the subject of your clothes? What have you to add?'

'I should really like to have a long dress and a woman's hat in order to go to church and take communion, and when I left, I should take them off. When I have carried out the work that God has sent me to do, then I shall wear women's clothes again.'

'What have you to add about your revelations?'

'I have them from God, without any other intermediary.'

He reminded her that she had said that the Archbishop of Rheims Charles de Bourbon and La Tremouille and others had seen the sign offered to Charles. Would they write their signatures on a letter to confirm this, saying that they had seen the sign? She found herself in a dilemma – many of them were not to be trusted. She said she was willing to write them a letter if he would provide a messenger to bring back an answer to her.

Finally she was invited to reflect on what had been said, and later having made no comments, was led back to her prison.

On May 9th nine men, the Abbot of Saint-Corneille, Compiegne, Master Jean de Chatillon and Guillaume Erard, Doctors of Holy Theology, André Marguerie and Nicholas de Venderès, Archdeacons of the Church of Rouen, Guillaume Haiton, bachelor of Holy Theology, Aubert Morel, licentiate of Canon Law, Nicholas Loiseleur, Canon of Rouen, and Jean Massieu, usher, took Jehanne to the torture chamber in the large tower of the castle.

One of the ecclesiastics told Jehanne that she had been brought here by order of the President, so that she could be put to torture to make her tell the truth about the lies she had been telling. Jehanne answered that even if they broke her bones she wouldn't change what she had said, and if they did force her to, she would say afterwards that it was only because she had been forced. Anyway, she had asked her Saints and they had said that God would help her.

'And I have asked my Saints if I shall be burned, and they have said I should talk to God about it, and he would help me.'

Another of the churchmen said to her, 'The sign of the crown which you said was handed to the Archbishop of Rheims, would you be willing to talk about this to this Pontiff?'

'Let him come here and I'll talk to him. He wouldn't dare contradict what I have said to you.'

At the end of the visit they decided that torture should be postponed for the time being. There is no doubt but that Cauchon had chosen these people with such a result in mind. It has been established that Jehanne is the only person who ever escaped being tortured in such circumstances. On May 12th a vote was taken after discussion and except for three of the assessors they agreed that it was unlikely that torture would produce any favourable result.

Quite early in the morning of Thursday May 24th 1431, Jehanne received an unexpected visitor, one of the members of the Tribunal who had been an active questioner. He came to give her an important piece of information from Cauchon: 'Today you must acknowledge our Holy Mother Church.'

Soon afterwards she was taken to the cemetery of the Saint-Ouen Abbey, where two platforms had been erected. One was a vast affair decorated with precious draperies, where the cardinal of Winchester with his secretary Callot were sitting with Cauchon, the bishops of Therouanne, de Noyon and Norwich, and some thirty members of the Tribunal. The other much smaller platform accommodated a number of other members of the Tribunal. Jehanne was taken there to stand near Guillaume Erard, one of Beauvais' most trusted familiars. The rest of the cemetery was packed with a crowd of spectators, hemmed in by English men-at-arms. In a corner was a cart occupied by the executioner and his assistants.

After Jehanne had arrived Erard began his sermon, taking as his text 'As the branch cannot bear fruit of itself, except it

166

abide in the vine; no more can ye, except ye abide in me.'
Having a reputation as a brilliant preacher to maintain, he
dealt with his subject at great length. Suddenly he was
horrified to notice that Jehanne was lost in an inner
contemplation, clearly communing with her Saints – not
listening to a word he was saying, and quite oblivious of her
surroundings. With all the forces of his lungs, and waving his
pointed finger at her face, he shouted, 'It is YOU I'm
addressing, Jehanne, and I tell you that your king is heretical
and schismatic!' The violence of his voice and invective jerked
her out of her reverie, and she shouted back: 'By my faith! I
dare swear that he is the noblest Christian among all the
Christians, and that he loves the faith and the Church more
than anyone!'

Fortunately for her, Erard had realized that she was in
enormous danger, being blissfully unaware that in a few
minutes she was to be condemned to death, and was about to
miss her cue!

Without responding to her exclamation Erard followed it
up by hurriedly enmeshing the high dignitaries before him,
saying, 'that the Lord Judges had often by word and deed
supported Our Holy Mother the Church, and there were
certain things which according to the judgment of clerics it is
not good to uphold . . .' when Jehanne suddenly interrupted
him, saying, 'I'm going to say something to you! Like anyone
owing obedience to the Church, I claim that everything I have
said and done should be sent to our Holy Father in Rome, to
whom, as to God, I will yield at once. As for everything I have
said and done, I have done it for the sake of God!'

The preacher tried in vain once more to get her to retract,
but again and again Jehanne repeated that she would only
yield to God and the pope. He made one last effort, saying that
they couldn't go and fetch His Holiness the Pope, he was so
great a distance away. And the ordinary bishops had judicial
rights in their own diocese.

'You must submit to the Church here!'

He repeated this three times, but Jehanne made no
response.

Cauchon rose up from his seat, and after an impressive
silence took the sentence out of his pocket and began to read
it. Jehanne meanwhile had reverted to her private medita-

tions, totally indifferent to her surroundings.

The minutes passed and the bishop continued his leisurely performance. A number of people surrounded her, and Erard offered her a Schedule of Renunciation, telling her over and over again to sign it.

Loyseleur implored her, 'Do what you're told, or you'll be dying today!'

Jean de Chatillon and Pierre Maurice added their voices. Everyone around her was saying, 'Do as you're told! Do you want to die?' And she still stayed immobile and withdrawn.

Cauchon's reading of the judgment was coming to its conclusion. Everyone observing him was well aware of his tactics, and suddenly Winchester's secretary burst out 'Hurry up! You're assisting the accused!' Cauchon seized his opportunity. Feigning furious anger he threw his papers down on the ground and shouted:

'You're a liar! My profession obliges me to seek the wellbeing of her soul as well as her body!'

'Traitor!' Callot shouted back.

'Apologize to me, or I shall refuse to continue any further!'

To bring the incident to a close, Winchester intervened telling his secretary to hold his tongue.

During this altercation Jehanne's pleaders at last got through to her and she suddenly called out at the top of her voice, 'Seeing that the Church people tell me that my apparitions and my revelation cannot be maintained or believed, I yield myself to my judges and to the Church!' and it is alleged that she added in a lower voice. 'I'd rather sign than be burned.'

Massieu immediately seized the Schedule of Renunciation Erard offered him. He at once read it out to her but probably she couldn't hear a word because of the tremendous noise that suddenly arose from the astounded crowd of onlookers. The text consisted of some eight lines, one of which contained a promise never to bear arms again, another to wear women's clothing forthwith, and a third to allow her hair to grow. Jehanne scribbled a circle containing a cross by way of signature, which she had explained during her interrogations to mean that whatever she had ostensibly agreed to, could be

168

ignored.

At the same time Cauchon took another paper out of his pocket, which he proceeded to read at great speed, this time it was the sentence to which the accused was now to be condemned:

TO LIFE IMPRISONMENT WITH THE BREAD
OF SORROW AND THE WATER OF ANGUISH

He had hardly finished reading this before a hail of stones hit the large platform. Not only had the result disappointed the crowd, but everyone who was near enough to see her remarked that she signed the paper with a false signature and she had a broad smile on her face, and some even thought that she laughed. Jehanne expected to be taken to an ecclesiastical prison, but to her surprise Massieu returned her to Bouvreuil. This was, of course, still another breach of canonical law, yet there was no single official complaint registered about it, even though there were three bishops and thirty canonical judges present. The other extraordinary infraction of the rules was the complete absence of any representative of the Inquisition!

16

Relapse and 'Execution'

As one would expect the journey back to Bouvreuil was by no means easy, the dignitaries and Jehanne had to be protected from the crowd, the English soldiers in particular being enraged at what had happened.

Remembering the various promises she had made in her Schedule of Renunciation, it is astonishing to learn that almost as soon as she was returned to her prison, she was obliged to cut off her hair! The obligation to wear women's clothes, however, was immediately enforced, and was followed by some disagreeable encounters with her jailers who attempted to take advantage of the opportunities they afforded to rape her. She managed to disappoint them as well as those of an English aristocrat who fancied his chances that night. As a result she was given chains – perhaps chain mail? – to protect herself at night. But four days later she put on her male clothes again.

On Monday May 28th Cauchon with seven of his assessors visited her and asked why she had taken again to wearing this forbidden attire. She replied it seemed to be more decorous, living amongst a lot of men. At the end of this interrogation, without prompting, she added that if the judges wanted her to, she would wear women's clothes again, and then pointed out that the promise made to her that if she did wear women's clothes she could attend mass and be allowed to take communion, had not been honoured. In any case, she continued, rather than spend her life in prison, she would prefer to die; four days had convinced her she would sooner be burned – no doubt influenced by her conviction that she could rely on her Voices when they said she would be liberated.

The following day Cauchon assembled his Tribunal members once more and informed them that Jehanne had reverted to her masculine garb, and asked them to give their opinions as to what should be done. Nicholas de Venderès, a reliable interpreter of Cauchon's wishes, immediately said he considered her to be a relapse and a heretic, and should suffer the penalties defined by canonical law and hand her over to the secular arm. He was followed by the Abbot of Fécamp who agreed in slightly different terms, and then the overwhelming majority of the forty-three assessors fell into line. The new sentence was drafted. As usual there was no representative of the Inquisition present, nor was Jean le Maître consulted before action was taken.

On Wednesday morning at seven o'clock, Jehanne was visited by Massieu and two Dominican friars, Ladvenu and Toutmouillé. Massieu then proceeded to read out the new sentence dated May 28th, given in the names of Pierre Cauchon and Jean le Maître, 'that the woman Jehanne commonly called la Pucelle, was to appear on the morrow, May 30th at eight o'clock in the morning, at the Old Market Place, Rouen, to be declared *relapse, excommunicant, and heretic.*'

I believe for the first time in her life Jehanne was utterly and completely shocked.

'Alas! Can people treat me so cruelly? Must my body, so lovely and so untouched, be burned today, reduced to cinders? . . . Ah! I would rather be beheaded seven times than burned like this!'

The promises of her Voices did not occur to her. She was without hope at this terrible moment. She stood alone, helpless, facing reality.

Suddenly she realized that if she were about to die, she must confess and be absolved. She begged Ladvenu to hear her, and though as an excommunicant she was not entitled to confess, he consented to listen and then, equally improperly, gave her absolution. Then she begged to be given the Eucharist, but this he felt unable to give her, saying that he would have to get permission from Cauchon – which he felt certain would be denied. However, Cauchon did not refuse, and Jehanne received her last communion, after which Ladvenu left. Toutmouillé stayed with her, but almost at once

Cauchon appeared. He told the friar that he wanted to be left alone with her to make one last effort to save her soul, and as the Dominican was leaving the room, he heard Jehanne bitterly accusing Cauchon:

'Bishop, it's because of you that I shall die!' and Cauchon replied as the friar shut the door:

'Ah Jehanne, be patient!'

It seems to be generally agreed that Jehanne at that time was imprisoned in the sizable circular ground floor dungeon of the only tower of Bouvreuil that still exists today. Access to the tower from the inner court of the castle was via a drawbridge leading to a passage that led to the dungeon door. To the right of this door inside the dungeon and the entrance to a spiral staircase leading up to the floor above, was a narrow dark recess some six feet deep, reached by a small level area leading down to two steps. There was an inconspicuous square trapdoor in the floor of the recess, giving access to a well of drinking water reached halfway down a long ladder fixed to the wall. At the bottom of the ladder there was an underground tunnel, which survives to this day and was used by the Gestapo to escape from the Allies in the Second World War. Jehanne, given a long hooded cloak, was taken to the ladder and at the bottom she was met by Haimond de Macy and another man who took her down the tunnel to the secret place where it would have ended. There three horses awaited them. Where they took her is not known. Everyone in Rouen being attracted to the Old Market Place, no one noticed her escape.

Meanwhile someone, probably Warwick, brought down the spiral staircase some 'real' witch, very likely one of the three called Jehanne who had already been condemned to death. She was dressed in the most extraordinary fashion, in a long black hooded cloak, her head covered by an enormous mitre which hid her face down to the end of her nose. A large placard bearing the words Heretic Relapse Witch was hung round her neck. She was handed over to the two friars and a score of guards who pushed her across the town to the Old Market Place, where she arrived almost an hour late. Meanwhile Cauchon was already installed there. The whole area of the Old Market Place surrounding the three platforms that had been erected, was crammed with some eight

172

hundred English men-at-arms who had pushed the ordinary spectators back into the side streets. Warwick had decreed that windows overlooking the Place should be shuttered. Probably these precautions were not made solely on account of the substitution of the victim for at that time La Hire and Gilles de Rais were both not far from Rouen with considerable forces, and an uprising of some of the inhabitants was deemed a possibility.

The largest of the three platforms that had been erected bore Cauchon, the bishops of Noyon and Norwich, the chancellor of France representing King Henry, Louis of Luxembourg, and the bishop of Therouanne who had earlier accompanied the delegation attempting to ransom Jehanne. But the dukes of Bedford and Warwick were both absent, and as usual there was no representative of the Inquisition.

On the second platform the bailiff of Rouen and his deputy were ready to take charge of the accused in accordance with canonical law, after she had been abandoned to the secular arm, because the Church was unable to inflict a death sentence.

Normally the victim was exposed to view to give an example to the crowd of what happened to witches, but here she was not to be seen from any angle, the hood covering even that part of her face below the mitre. She stood on the third platform near Nicholas Midy, (a canon of Rouen for less than a fortnight) who had been entrusted with the sermon which was based on the text 'and whether one member suffer, all the members suffer with it', indicating the nature of the judgment Cauchon was about to give. At the end of it Cauchon solemnly read the sentence declaring 'Jehanne, commonly called the Maid, heretical, schismatic, invoker of demons, idolatress, blasphemous of the name of God, and contemptuous of the saints of divine law and the sacraments' to which the condemned woman made no denial. One cannot but imagine how vehemently Jehanne would have protested!

Cauchon continued that she had refallen into heresy as the dog returns to its vomit, and in order to prevent the infection of other people she was to be abandoned to the secular arm, but he prayed them to moderate his judgment in not mutilating her limbs before death, as usually happened. This was essential to Cauchon as she would have been stripped of

173

her clothes and her absence of scars would have shown the executioner it was not Jehanne la Pucelle he was about to burn!

But before she could be transferred to the secular arm there had to be the Sacrament of Penitence, and once more the long recital of her wickednesses was intoned. When at last this was over all the ecclesiastics except Ladvenu and another friar Ysembart retired, and the Bailiff is alleged to have said to his guards, 'You can go away!' So contrary to the usual practice she was NOT handed over to the secular arm, which presumably accounts for the interesting fact that no written record of the execution of Jehanne la Pucelle appears in any of the Rouen archives, nor indeed that any execution at all took place on May 30th 1431! In fact the unfortunate woman was at once seized by the soldiers and unceremoniously chained to the stake, and the fuel forthwith set on fire. After she was dead the soldiers broke their ranks and the executioner exposed to the crowd what was left of the witch, proving that it was a woman who had been burned. The corpse was put back on the fire and ultimately after four hours the cinders were thrown into the Seine. No one knows to this day the identity of the woman who was burned.[16]

On June 7th an official document called *Informatio post executionem* was published, giving an account of the interview that was alleged to have taken place when Cauchon was left alone with the Maid in her dungeon on the morning of the execution. After repeating the remarks which Toutmouillé heard before he shut the door, the conversation is supposed to have continued: 'You are dying because you have not kept your promises.' This document was added to various papers concerning the trial by Cauchon.

On June 8th a letter from Henry VI was sent out to the Emperor and the sovereigns of Europe to announce the death of the Maid of Orleans and on June 28th the bishops and heads of towns occupied by English soldiers were also informed. None of the letters makes any reference to how she died, nor mentions any ecclesiastical or legal document signed by any judicial authority.

Not surprisingly there was a great deal of scepticism at the time that the Maid had in fact been burned, though there seem to have been no rumours about her whereabouts.

There is a manuscript in the British Museum, No 11,542 which says: 'She was burned publicly, or some other woman like her, of which many people have had and still have diverse opinions.' And the *Chronique bretonne* announced 'In the year 1431 the Maid was burned in Rouen, or condemned to be.' The Bourgeois of Paris in his Journal quoted the opinion of many of his contemporaries: 'many firmly believed that by her saintliness she escaped the fire and that they burned someone else believing it was she.' Perhaps the neatest and certainly the most reliable summing up is that of Saint-Thibaud de Metz 'one reads that in the city of Rouen in Normandy, she was burned on a fire, but later the contrary was proven.'

17

Her Life After Her 'Execution'[17]

William Caxton, who was born in Kent in 1422, wrote in his Chronicle of England, published in 1480, that he had learned whilst on a journey in France that Jehanne had been kept a prisoner for nine months after her supposed execution. Various suggestions of her whereabouts have been put forward – that she was imprisoned in the castle at Crotoy which was in the hands of the English, or she was held in some Burgundian stronghold, or she took refuge with Colette de Corbie in the convent which was her headquarters at Besançon, but as far as I know there is no documentation to support these ideas.

Some intriguing scraps of evidence have been uncovered however, which may reveal her possible whereabouts for some five years after her condemnation in Rouen. It is suggested that the Duchess of Bedford persuaded her husband to have Jehanne conducted by the two young men who had met her in the subterranean passage, to some place where she was mercifully and comfortably immured. Now the Duchess died in Rouen in 1432, nine months after the 'execution', and it may be the Duke – possibly in response to a dying wish of his wife – then liberated Jehanne in exchange for a promise that she would leave France, would not fight against the English, and would live under an assumed name. Bernard-Jean Daulon, a descendant of Jean d'Aulon, Jehanne's militant has suggested that the only Court which might have been prepared to welcome her, was that of the Pope.

When Jehanne was captured, the reigning pope was Martin V who had been elected in 1417 thanks to the able advocacy of

Cauchon. It is said that Martin was devoted to Yolande. His secretary Morosini mentioned in his chronicles that there had been a correspondence between the pope and Charles VII. Martin died in 1431 soon after Jehanne had wished to appeal to him. The new pope was Eugene IV, elected on April 29th 1431. His secretary was Silvius Piccolomini (who later became Pope Pius II), and he wrote in his memoirs apropos of Jehanne's visions: 'Whether these were divine or human I should find it hard to say. This epic could have been an expedient, thought up by one of the princes in the French Court, the most wise one, in order to rally all the courageous spirits throughout France in support of that one which had been sent by God.'

One wonders how generally Yolande's influence was so clearly recognized at that time, for surely it was she who was meant. It certainly suggests that there was a leak about that discussion when the shepherdess myth was put forward.

It does seem very reasonable to suppose that Pope Eugene would have welcomed Jehanne to his Court, sympathetic as she was to his ideas concerning a united Christendom. At that time too he was in difficulties because certain princes and subjects were staging an armed revolt against him. According to the Bourgeois de Paris (Page 355) 'she went dressed as a man, and was a soldier for the Holy Father Eugene, and twice committed homicide in the said war.'

The Duke of Bedford died on September 14th 1435. This would have meant that Jehanne felt herself relieved of her promises to leave France and not fight against the English. It seems that she managed to get into touch with her two foster brothers and arranged to meet them on May 20th 1436 at La Grange-aux-Ormes, a small place quite close to Metz where there was a castle-cum-farm owned by an aristocratic Metzian family. She turned up dressed as a woman and going by the name of Claude, a name applicable to either sex.

It is interesting to consider why she chose to reappear there. At that time Metz was an important small republic with a high reputation. The Third Order was strongly organized there. It was politically completely independent of France, Lorraine, and the Holy Roman Empire. The city was divided into five districts, called *paraiges* which took it in turn to appoint one of their citizens to be governor for a year. The head personage met the most powerful princes of Europe on an equal footing. It had its own courts of justice, and coined its own money. It may be remembered that after Charles's coronation Nicholas Louve had been knighted at Jehanne's request, the sole recipient of such a signal honour. He served his turns as governor of Metz.

Another noteworthy citizen at that time was an enthusiastic diarist, who was mayor of Saint Thibaud and vicar of Saint Eucaire. He recorded the events occurring there on a day-to-day basis for many years until 1445 when he is assumed to have died. He wrote 'The year MCCCCXXXVI Sire Phelepin Marcoulz was the governor of Metz. This year on XXth of May came the Maid Jehanne who had been in France, to La Grange-aux-Ormes, near Saint-Privey, and she had come there to talk with certain gentlemen of Metz, and she called herself Claude, and the same day she came to see her two brothers there, one was a knight and called himself Pierre, and the other an equerry, called Petit Jean, and they had believed that she had been burned, and as soon as they saw her they recognized her, and also she recognized them, and the Monday XXIst day of that May they took their sister with them to Bacquillin, and Sir Nicole Lowe knight gave her a horse costing XXX francs and a pair of gaiters, and Sir Aubert Boulay a hood, and Sire Nicole Groingnait a sword, and the said Maid jumped onto the said horse very cleverly, and said many things to the said Nicole Lowe from which he understood that it was she who had been in France who had taken to be crowned the king Charles at Rheims, and they wanted to say many times that how they believed she had been burned in Rouen in Normandy, and she spoke about other things mostly in parables and did not speak of her escape nor her intentions and said she had lost all her power before Saint John the Baptist's Day'. The diarist continued saying she went to 'the town of Marieuville and stayed there about three weeks, and she made a pilgrimage to Nostre-Dame de Liance.' And he continued 'When she wanted to go many people in Metz came to see her at the said Marieuville, and there they gave her many jewels and they recognized that it was the real Jehanne the Maid of France, and Joffroy Dex gave her a horse and then they went to Arelont, a town that is in the duchy of Lucembourg.'

She was accompanied by her two 'brothers' on these journeys and on her pilgrimage to the Black Virgin at Liesse. Here a special confraternity had been established by the French royal family for the princes and princesses of royal blood. The three went next to Arlon, which was then the capital of Luxembourg. Here Jehanne's aunt, Elizabeth of Luxembourg, widow of Antoine de Bourgogne and an aunt of Philippe le Bon, welcomed them and they stayed with her for more than five months. While there, Jehanne was invited to visit Cologne by the Count of Virnenbourg, and was escorted there by the son of her host. It is pleasant to suppose that her knowledge of the German dialect spoken in the Lorraine countryside proved valuable on this occasion. It is said that she hoped that his father might introduce her to the Emperor, in order to discuss on behalf of the Pope the possibility of mounting a new crusade to the Holy Land. Her host, who was greatly taken with her, presented her with a handsome cuirass. But while she was there, two clerics were disputing for the bishopric of Troyes and Jehanne rashly took sides in the argument. She found herself as a result viewed with suspicion by the local representative of the Inquisition, Henri Kaltiser, the General of Mayence, who demanded that she should come to see him. She hurriedly left Cologne and returned to Arlon, once more travelling under the protection of the young heir of Virnenbourg.

The archivist of the State of Luxembourg recently discovered three safe-conducts issued at Cologne in July and August 1436, one is in the name of Pucelle de France.

Soon after her return to Arlon she became engaged to be married to Robert des Armoises, Lord of Tichemont, a young widower, member of a distinguished aristocratic family. He was a cousin of Robert de Baudricourt's wife. It is not impossible that Jehanne and he had met at the Baudricourt wedding in Vaucouleurs when Jehanne would have been about eighteen. Jehanne had received several proposals of marriage in the interval and had invariably turned them down on the grounds of her vow of virginity as long as God required her to keep it. Possibly Robert des Armoises had been hard to forget and meeting him again had been no disappointment. Almost certainly her Saints had told her that her long lasting prohibition had now been lifted, for the third item in her

mission – the restoration of Paris to Charles – had triumph-
antly been achieved by Richemont and Dunois a month
before she had reappeared in La Grange-des-Ormes. If she
had indeed fought for the Pope in Italy this might well have
stood her in good stead in the eyes of Heaven as well, and no
crusade was in the offing.

Whether her future husband knew that he would be
marrying someone who was physically incapable of having
sexual intercourse unless a miracle occurred, I do not know.
Jehanne's faith may well have been so absolute that she had
not thought it necessary to tell him. Her confidence in her
Saints' promises must have been unquestionable after her
escape from Rouen. Possibly Robert had been told and his
faith was as great as hers, indeed, what consequently
happened might seem to confirm this. That she was fully
aware that she needed to be changed is hardly to be
doubted.

Jehanne wrote a great number of letters while she was in
Arlon, and Petit Jean spent much of his time travelling
between Arlon and Orleans, Loches and Blois delivering
them and bringing answers back. One of her letters arriving
on July 25th was addressed to Guillaume le Bellier who had
visited the Duke of Orleans in London in 1429, and whose
wife had looked after Jehanne's establishment in Chinon.
One wonders if this was to ask him to inform her exiled
stepbrother the Duke of Orleans of her reappearance and
proposed marriage.

The following details of some of her correspondence are to
be found in the meticulously kept accounts in the archives of
Orleans:

On August 5th the king received Petit Jean and a party of
four horsemen who had come with him to Orleans, bringing a
letter from his sister. He received them with kindness and
made them a present of a hundred francs, which they were
paid on August 21st. 'Given to Fleur de Lys, the city's Herald
at Arms, the sum of two gold *réaulx* on August 9th for bringing
letters to the city from Jehanne.' Fleur de Lys had been one of
the captains in her company fighting in 1429.

The king took advantage of this meeting to tell Petit Jean
that in future Jehanne and Pierre and himself should have the
surname du Lys, and it seems that after this they all availed

themselves of the royal coat of arms granted after the relief of Orleans to Jehanne la Pucelle only. It had not previously been used, though when she was asked about this coat of arms during the trial, she said it had been given to her brothers by the king 'for their pleasure.'

'September 2nd. Passage to Orleans of a messenger, Coeur de Lys, Herald-at-Arms, also carrying letters from the Maid to the king.'

'October 18th. To the same messenger was paid for a journey which he had made for the same city of Orleans for letters in his possession for the Maid, who was at Arlon, in the duchy of Luxembourg, and to carry the said letters from the said Jehanne the Maid to Loches, where the king had gone to be near the queen Marie and her son, on which journey he had been away forty one days, that is to say thirty four days on the journey to the Maid and seven days to go to Loches and then to go to the said Maid the last Tuesday in July and returned September 2nd following, for this 6 l.p.'

Six days after the arrival of Jehanne's first letter on July 25th, the city of Orleans sent a messenger who had been one of her companions-in-arms to see the king. He left Orleans on September 2nd and perhaps he represented the city at her marriage which probably took place in October in the Duchess's chapel in the castle at Arlon.

The Metz diarist wrote: 'At Arlon the marriage took place of Sir Robert des Armoises, knight, and the said Jehanne la Pucelle,[18] and then the said Lord of Armoises and his wife went to live in Metz in the house of the said Sir Robert which he had facing Saint Segolene, and they stayed there as long as they pleased.' It seems they normally lived there during the winter but spent the summers in their castle at Jaulny.[19] In this castle which is near Thiacourt in Meurthe and Moselle, there are two delightful portraits in a recess over the mantelpiece in the large salon, of Jehanne and her husband looking at one another. They are in excellent condition having been hidden for many years. The panels surrounding the circular portraits are decorated with dolphins. There are also twinned coats of arms of the Armoises and of Jehanne la Pucelle in the salon.

It had been made very clear to Jehanne that she was not going to be welcomed back at Court. Nobody there wanted any radical changes to take place in society, and the church considered her supposed execution much less disturbing than her reappearance at Court would be. The English were no longer the serious threat that they had been, for Richemont and Dunois were managing to continue the good work that she had started. Yolande had persuaded Burgundy at long last to break with the English, and in 1435 he signed the Treaty of Arras, though it involved paying him 50,000 ecus for the pleasures lost by Jean sans Peur because he had been assassinated! And they undertook to construct an expiatory chapel where he had lost his life, and to hold masses there for the lamented victim. They handed over the earldoms of Auxerre, Bar-sur-Seine, Mâcon and others, and various towns including Mondidier, Peronne and Saint-Quentin, (which places were already under his control); they dispensed with receiving his homage; and they undertook to support him against the fury of the English at his defection! It was characteristic of Yolande's far-sighted wisdom, that in spite of the apparent one-sidedness of the Treaty of Arras, Burgundy's influence steadily diminished from this time on, while the king's power as steadily increased.

Absolutely no mention of Jehanne's name is found in any official French document from the time of her supposed execution until after her real death! Not even the fact that she had apparently been executed, except only that she had died.

Jehanne and her husband after spending their honeymoon in Arlon, went to Metz, just as the diarist wrote, but very soon one learns with surprise that so far from settling down together, Jehanne is leaving her newly wedded husband and going off to the wars again. I cannot believe this is due to Jehanne's love of fighting, as is usually assumed. I think rather it is because no miracle took place, and having discussed it with her disappointed husband they came to the conclusion that Heaven felt Jehanne had somehow made a mistake in believing she had done all that was required of her.

They let about a quarter of the land he owned to some friends. The lease which is still extant, concerns the domain of Haraucourt, and was signed on November 7th 1436 by 'Robert des Armoises, Lord of Tichemont, and Jehanne du Lys, La Pucelle de France, Lady of the said Tichemont, my

Jehanne la Pucelle

Jehanne's Royal coat of arms

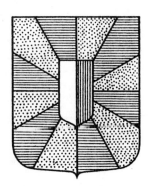

Robert's coat of arms

Robert des Armoises

The coats of arms in the Salon at the Castle in Jaulny

wife, to Colard de Failly, equerry of Marville, and his wife Poisinette, for 350 *francs lorrains.*' The money they obtained was spent in fitting out Jehanne once more as a warrior and providing her with a small company of mercenaries. A month later she and Pierre set out for Tiffauges, where Gilles de Rais welcomed her. Meanwhile Robert entered the strictly celibate Celestine monastery in Metz where he stayed until she returned.

At this time Gilles de Rais was a chamberlain of the king as well as his marshal. I imagine Charles and Yolande, told of Jehanne's dilemma, had given their consent to her co-operating in clearing the countryside of the terrible *Ecorcheurs (Flayers),* and if she came across some English troops, one would hardly expect her to resist getting rid of them too, if it were feasible, especially as Gilles had undertaken to provide her with the necessary troops at his expense. But it must be understood that there would be no official recognition by, or connection with, the Court.

Gilles showed his pleasure at having her company again by staging a performance of the inordinately extravagant 'Mystery of the Siege of Orleans'. This was a spectacular theatrical pageant, involving 500 actors sumptuously dressed, reciting 20,000 lines of verse re-enacting the liberation of Orleans and the heroic part played by la Pucelle. It was designed to evoke the glorious hours that Orleans had experienced at that time. The whole population was invited to partake of free hospitality at his expense. It cost a fortune to produce.

Later they set out together to clean up the numerous gangs of unemployed mercenaries, soldiers and hordes of bandits who were making life a misery in many parts of the surrounding country, which were preventing any serious reconstruction and restoration of prosperity.

When they had pacified the countryside Jehanne and Gilles carried out successful campaigns in the Gironde, which was still held by the English, and they mounted a siege of Bordeaux with strong support from artillery, and this was followed by the liberation of the Bayonne. Evidence of these campaigns is available because a Bohemian judge, a brother-in-law of the Bohemian king, had travelled that year to Bordeaux and wrote about his experiences. And in the

Chartres treasury there is a letter addressed to the king by an equerry from Gascoigne asking for a remission of a sentence passed upon him for having plundered some villages in Anjou, because he had helped a woman called Jehanne, who was said to be la Pucelle, to retake Le Mans which had been occupied by the English. Letters of complaint were also sent at that time to the English authorities from English people living in Bordeaux complaining that strong forces were being deployed against them, so they were thinking of returning to England.

Later, in 1439, Jehanne was seriously wounded near Poitou and gave up her commandment to Jean de Siquenville.

After Jehanne's supposed execution in Rouen, a procession and masses for the repose of her soul had been held every May 8th in Orleans until 1436 when it was learned that she was alive and well. Then, on the eve of Corpus Christi 1439 eight masses were reinstituted for the 'Obsequies of the late Jehanne la Pucelle' as rumour had convinced the city once more that she was dead. But fortunately she broke her journey on the way back to Lorraine to visit Orleans. She was rapturously received. On July 18th the accounts show an entry by the financial controller for a celebratory wine party, when she was given a silver platter containing a large number of gold coins – IICXX *livres parises* – as a gift in recognition of her services during the siege. Further jollifications were held on July 28th and 29th, and she left on August 1st, but returned again on September 4th.

Meanwhile the king had arrived in Orleans on August 25th, and Yolande as well. The king was staying in the same house as the Maid – where Jehanne had stayed before. There are eight entries in the 'Register of the Accounts of the Fortress' written by one Morschoasne, dealing with her visit. These three are typical:

'To Jacquet Leprestre, the 18th day of July, for ten pints and a half of wine presented to Lady Jehanne des Armoises , for this 14 *sols parisis.'*

'To the said Jacquet the penultimate day of July, for meat bought at Basin, Pierre Sévin there, to present to my said Lady Jehanne des Armoises. . .'

'To Jehanne des Armoises for a gift for her . . .
agreed by the City Council for the good that she did
for the city during the siege . . . IICCXX *livres
parisis.'*

Jehanne went away for some weeks after August 1st, but
returned on September 4th. The King's Council was there –
Dunois, Charles d'Anjou, Lord de Chaumont, the archbishop of Vienne, and Rabateau, (with whom she had stayed
in Poitiers.) They and a crowd of other guests were in the
garden of the House of the Annunciation, when Jehanne
arrived back. The king, as once before, made himself as
inconspicuous as possible, and then suddenly found a
beautiful creature with short hair standing before him. No
one doubted but that he was looking at the miraculous
shepherdess. And according to his chamberlain, de Boissy, he
said: 'Pucelle, my friend, it is well for you to come once more
in the name of God who knows our secret, which is between
you and me.'

Whereupon she went down on her knees before him,
realizing that this really was her moment of lasting renunciation.

But there is evidence that letters still passed between them.
The archives of Tours mention on 'October 29th the payment
to a messenger, Jean Drouat, for his journey of September
27th to Orleans to take sealed letters which the Bailiff had
written to the king concerning the Lady of Armoises and a
letter he had received from the said Jehanne for the same
gentleman.

When Jehanne reached Metz her husband left the monastery and they lived together thereafter, mostly spending the
winters in the town and their summers in the castle at Jaulny.
The family of his younger brother who adopted de Sermoise
as his surname, much later lived at d'Autrey, some forty miles
from Jaulny, not far from Nancy. Jehanne became the
godmother of her eldest nephew, for whom she chose the
name of Louis. It is interesting to learn that the eldest son of
the family was nearly always called Louis after that, although

The Castle at Jaulny

they had never used it before. Her thwarted maternal instincts found a great satisfaction in this relationship, and she seems to have spent a great deal of time in his company frequently riding over to their house (it is not known where it was) on one of her horses.

A new church was being built in the adjacent town of Pulligny-en-Madon, in the new Gothic style. Jehanne provided much of the money required to complete and decorate the interior. She wished to be buried there with her husband, and when she died in 1449, probably of a fever, she was interred inside the church to the right of the altar. It is said she was buried with her rings and jewels and the golden spurs that Charles had given her. Her husband died a year later, and he was buried in the same grave, dressed in his armour. The builder of the church was earlier assigned a sepulchre to the left of the altar.

At the end of the seventeenth century the lettering on the tombstone had begun to get effaced by the feet of the faithful, so the descendant of her godson erected a plaque on a wall adjacent to their tomb which pointed out where Jehanne and her husband were buried. In 1890 at a time when the

188

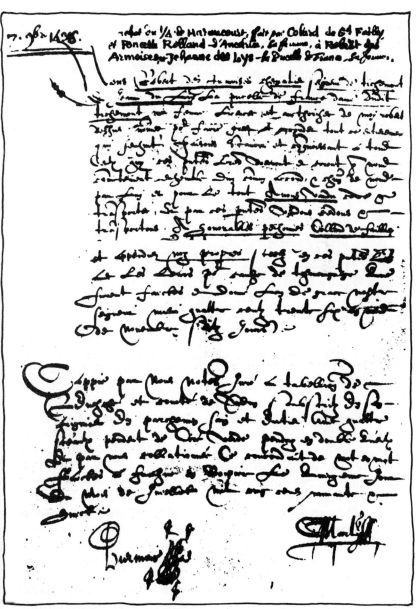

The Lease of Haraucourt signed on November 7th 1436 by Robert des Armoises, Lord of Tichemont and Jehanne du Lys, la Pucelle de France, Lady of the said Tichemont, and Colard de Failly equerry de Marville and his wife Poisinette for 350 *francs lorrains*.

preliminaries for the beatification of Joan of Arc were in progress, some iconoclasts cemented over their tombstone and covered it with kitchen tiles and then tore down the plaque. But the mouldings framing it were overlooked, and they can still be seen on the adjacent wall which has recently been repaired.

One Saturday afternoon in November 1968, Count Pierre de Sermoise, a descendant of Jehanne's brother-in-law, went to the church with three interested friends to meet the mayor of Pulligny, Monsieur Girot, and one of the inhabitants of the

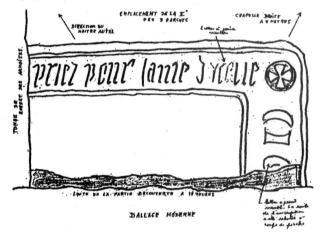

Sketch by Guerillon of the exposed part of Jehanne's tomb

town, an old master mason called Monsieur Florentin. Having lived there all their lives these two knew every detail of the history of the tomb as well as its exact site. They said that the coat of arms of the Maid had been carved on the keystone of the ribbed vault, but it had been scraped away during the Revolution. Thanks to the willing cooperation of the vicar, the Abbot Chrétien, the party was allowed to attempt to expose the tombstone. After two hours of hard work an area was loosened, and the corner of the tomb appeared, freed of cement. It carried a Gothic inscription which they could identify. It was typical of the fifteenth century. It was clearly one of the oldest sepulchres in the church, (though it was not mentioned in the contemporary guide.) Some words, partially worn away, were followed by a sign which though incomplete

190

they recognized as the cross with equal arms within a circle, characteristic of the Franciscan movement. Jehanne had first seen it on her ring engraved with the words Jhesus-Marie, and it was on the standard which found itself in the cathedral during the coronation of Charles VII.

PRIEZ POUR LAME D   LLE   CI

The rest of the lettering which was uncovered had been deliberately defaced by a mattock. Before further removal of the cement could be carried out the bishop ordered it all to be replaced at once. The sketch was made by Guérillon at the time.

EPILOGUE

After Pierre and Petit Jean had recognized Jehanne they received a number of royal favours. Petit Jean who was already in the king's service was rapidly promoted to be chamberlain to the king, captain of Chartres, bailiff of Vermandois and by the following October, provost of Vaucouleurs. Pierre was elected a member of the prestigious Order of the Porcupine – an order similar to and founded to rival that of the Order of the Garter. This order had a limited number of members, and was only open to people whose family had been noblemen for at least four generations. This proves that the Darcs had borne arms for a long time and that Jacques had been privately restored by the king to the aristocracy subsequent to his derogation.

In 1439 Charles VII had granted Pierre du Lys payment as a bailiff of Chaumont which gave him quite a substantial income. From the beginning of 1440 he lived in Orleans. From July 7th of the same year Isabelle Romée also lived there, the city having granted her a pension and they looked after her when she was ill. There are entries in the accounts for her nurses and helpers. She lived in the *Rue des Pastoreaux.* The payments were made to the 'mother of Jehanne la Pucelle' until 1449; in 1450 they were changed to the 'mother of the late Jehanne la Pucelle'. Isabelle herself died on November 25th 1458.

In 1439 negotiations began between the English and French kings to bring hostilities to an end. The man in charge was Pierre Cauchon, the Bishop of Beauvais. In 1440 the Convention of Westminster was signed on July 2nd, and Charles, Duke of Orleans, was repatriated against a ransom of 120,000 golden crowns. He marked his appreciation of Pierre du Lys's services by giving him and his son Jehan 'the fruits, profits, usufructs, revenues and emoluments of an island situated in the river Loire . . . This Isle-des-Boeufs has been given by the said Duke to the said Pierre in compensation for the loss of the goods of his wife, sold in order to pay for his ransom, and for his loyalty in leaving his land to serve the king our lord and the duke in the company of Jehanne la Pucelle, HIS SISTER, with whom until her absence *(son absentment)* he jeopardized himself in her service.' (my emphasis). The use of the word absence is highly significant, defining as it does the state of not being present, but still not implying that she was dead. And later in the document they repeat the words *Jehanne la Pucelle, sa soeur,* and *dite Pucelle, sa soeur germaine.* At the same time Jehanne is called neither Darc nor du Lys. Further sums of money were granted by way of pension to Jehan the son of Pierre, after his father had died.

When Jehanne and her secrets were safely buried, Charles decided the time had come to remove any suggestion that he owed his throne to witchcraft or a heretic. Though the term 'so-called dauphin' had long been forgotten, the stigma that a not unimportant part of the Church – the Tribunal of Rouen approved by the University of Paris – had decreed that his coronation was thanks to 'that creature in the form of a woman who had been condemned as a heretic, witch, and relapse' still remained, and it offered a potential threat to the Valois dynasty.

With little difficulty in 1449 his army, reorganized by Richemont, threw the English out of Rouen and Charles immediately took possession of every ecclesiastical archive he could lay his hands on there. Then he approached the pope and requested him to overturn the shameful sentence passed on Jehanne la Pucelle.

All kinds of difficulties emerged. The Inquisition denied their responsibility because they had taken no part in the trial – and it was true that Graverand had not been present at a single session. Yet on July 4th 1431 he had given a sermon, full of contradictions and obscurities, approving of her death at the stake. The University of Paris could only produce two relevant letters, but one (inspired by Bedford) from King Henry, was not within the Inquisition's province since the king was not a religious. The abjuration that Jehanne had signed with a cross in a circle was not to be found. Some of the sheets recording what had been said at her trial lacked the signatures of the notaries affirming that they were a true record. Most of the originals were lacking anyway, and quite a lot of the Latin translation, regarded as the official record, was obscure and ambiguous, though for lack of anything else it was adopted as the official version of the trial by Charles.

Since 1431 there had been a big change in the attitude of the University. When the capital welcomed Charles back as sovereign in 1436, he tactfully let bygones be bygones. But in 1450 it became clear that he was about to take a hard line towards anyone defending the Tribunal's condemnation of Jehanne, whereupon no fewer than seven senior members of the late Cauchon's most reliable supporters were amongst the first to rally to Charles's dynastic cause.

This was not hard to understand, as Cauchon, or other interested parties, had apparently managed to eliminate whoever and whatever might have given those important secrets away. Of the eighty assessors who had been involved with the trial only ten now survived! The Bishop of Coutances had suddenly died in 1431. Pierre Loiseleur, who had fled to Basle was found dead unexpectedly. La Fontaine disappeared. Jehan d'Estivet was found drowned in a pond. The inquisitor Jean le Maître 'evaporated' . . . It is hard to believe that even in those unhealthy days, all these occurrences were purely coincidental.

A former rector of the University of Paris was asked to institute an inquiry into the validity of Jehanne's trial, and to get statements from such witnesses as he should think proper. He chose Guillaume Manchon, the chief of the three notaries who had recorded the trial, and produced the formal Latin version – falsified where required by Cauchon; Jean Massieu, the usher who had taken Jehanne from her prison to the various sessions, and then back again; Jean Beaupère, a scholar who had asked Jehanne a multitude of questions at the interrogations; Ladvenu the friar who had confessed her and was allowed to give her communion when she believed she was about to be executed; Isambard de la Pierre, who had accompanied the 'real witch' to the Old Market Place, believing her to be Jehanne; Guillaume Duval, a Dominican friar who had attended many of the court sessions; and another Dominican Jean Toutmouillé who left her in the prison cell alone with Cauchon when he made his 'last attempt' to save her.

The report these people produced after careful consideration said that the original trial was null and void, but nothing further happened, presumably it was pigeonholed at the Vatican. The pope, Nicolas V, who certainly knew all the facts, was unsympathetic. Although France was alleged to be 'the eldest daughter of the Church', Rome turned a deaf ear to Charles's appeals year after year, justifying the delay because his energies were taken up by the serious Turkish threat to Christianity. (In addition he had no wish to antagonize the English just then, for hopes of persuading them to mount a new crusade.) In 1452 the pope's legate Guillaume d'Estouteville continued to press Charles's petition, and he managed to gain an ally in the then Inquisitor of France, Jean Bréhal, by revealing the real reason for Charles's persistence – that the English after capturing the simple and pure Jehanne la Pucelle, seriously managed to damage His Majesty's honour by staging her trial on a matter of faith, and then condemning her to a shameful death for heresy and witchcraft.

At that time the Eastern Roman empire was crumbling and disturbing signs in England and Germany were also appearing, undermining the unity of the Faith. Bréhal saw an opportunity here and made great efforts to convince the pope that by acceding to Charles's request, he could in this way firmly seal for the present, perhaps for ever, the unity of faith of the Church's eldest daughter. A second inquiry took place undertaken by the papal legate in France when twenty-one witnesses were examined in Rouen, but again nothing official followed. Bréhal had been finally convinced of how worthwhile a settlement of the matter would be, when in December 1452 he received a generous gift of thirty seven *livres* in golden crowns from Charles to cover any expenses he might incur in persuading the pope of this. To ease the pope's conscience Bréhal explained, 'We do not have to fathom these secrets of which everyone is ignorant, and which were known only to the king and the Maid. It is not for us to probe with too great a concern as to why they have hidden these mysterious secrets!'

But in spite of his efforts Bréhal failed to help Charles until

1455 when Alphonse Borgia, after waiting for many years, at last became pope, calling himself Calixtus III. He immediately acceded to Charles's request but introduced two interesting modifications. The name Jehanne la Pucelle was dropped and replaced by Jeanne Darc, and the Darc family instead of King Charles was officially regarded as begging to have Jehanne rehabilitated. The significance of these changes were twofold. It minimized the fact that the main beneficiary of the action would be Charles, and members of the Darc family would not be required to take an oath swearing to tell the truth if testifying to the court.

The Pope named as commissioners in charge of the inquiry, Jean Jouvenal, the Archbishop of Rheims, Guillaume Chartier the Bishop of Paris, Richard de Longeuil the Bishop of Coutances, and Master Jean Bréhal Inquisitor of the Faith.

According to Oursel, the morning of November 7th 1455 saw these gentlemen (except for Longeuil) accompanied by a large crowd of clergy and laity, men and women, assemble in the Cathedral of Notre Dame in Paris.

'Suddenly, uttering groans and sighs Isabelle Darc, widow of the late Jacques Darc, and mother of Jeanne, (sic), commonly called la Pucelle, thrust herself towards the commissioners and humbly prostrating herself in front of them proceeded to read out a formal document written by Pope Calixtus, which she held in her hand, describing her sad and pitiful request: 'Through my legitimate marriage I had a daughter; she was baptized and duly confirmed; I brought her up in the fear of God, in respect for the tradition of the Church as far as her age and our condition permitted; living amongst the animals and the work of the farm, she frequented the church not a little, but very often, and she observed the sacraments of communion and penitence every month; she prayed and fasted with fervour for the miseries of these times, and she pitied people with all her heart. She had never thought or done anything contrary to our faith.

'Nevertheless, my Jeanne was dragged by the enemies of the kingdom before the law, and they condemned her to the stake, and the defilement of it has besmirched us all! Until it pleases the divine Mercy to give us back, after the clouds, the blue sky; after the war, peace; after the darkness, light; to

196

restore the city of Rouen, then all of Normandy to their rightful lord, and to complete at last that which in the time of Jeanne had been undertaken, first at Orleans and then as at Rheims.'

'Weeping, the lady Isabelle prostrated herself before the high personages, gave them the document and asked for justice.'

The Darc family was legally represented by Master Guillaume Prévosteau and Master Pierre Maugier. The two Darc sons explained they were unable to attend the sessions on account of their work!

I must confess to feeling very surprised by the alleged behaviour of Isabelle Romée. It seems to me so completely out of character. Surely Isabelle Romée would never have agreed to claim that she had given birth to Jehanne? But perhaps she had been informed of the 'right of mental restriction'? Might she have been told that the Pope ordered her to read out what he had written? I do wonder, however, since she was in her seventies by that time and in poor health, whether someone else did not impersonate her, perhaps without her knowledge, particularly as Prévosteau said early in his introduction, 'because though lying is forbidden, to hide the truth may be permitted, in proper time and place, by means of fictitious or circumlocutory expressions.'!

However, I do not regard a critical account of the Rehabilitation Trial as part of Jehanne's biography. It is of interest only because a great deal of hearsay as well as direct evidence was presented to it. Lists of questions were answered by some thirty-four people living in Domremy, who had known Jehanne when she was living there. Then people who had known her because of the trial in Rouen, or from her time spent in Orleans, testified. And lastly people who had belonged to her household or had taken part in her campaigns were questioned as to her character and behaviour. On the whole I believe people answered honestly so it makes interesting reading, but Dunois, the Bastard, who had become a close friend and confidant to the king, embroidered his answers quite a lot in order to provide evidence to show that Jehanne undoubtedly had been sent by God to relieve Orleans and bring about the coronation of Charles in Rheims. The final contribution to the inquiry was a long straightforward account by her militant d'Aulon, of her courage, piety and godliness. Though he had seen her naked he had not been excited by it. She never swore. He believed she had been sent by God.

The questions put to the inhabitants of Domremy are as follows:

1. Place of origin and parish of the Maid.
2. Her parents. Their condition. If they were good Christians, and of good reputation.
3. Her godfathers and godmothers.
4. If while a child she had been reared in the faith as required by her age and condition.
5. Her comportment during adolescence from the age of seven to her leaving home.
6. If she willingly frequented the church and its saints.
7. Her occupation while she was young.
8. If at that time she confessed willingly and often.
9. 'The Tree of the Fairies'. If young girls went there to dance. The spring nearby. Did Jehanne go there with the other girls and when?
10. Her leaving and her journey.
11. Where was he (the person answering) when inquiries were being made at the time when she was being detained by the English after her capture at Compiegne?
12. When there was an evacuation to Neufchateau on account of the war was Jehanne always accompanied by her mother and father?

These questions were asked when the first (abortive) inquiry was held. It is interesting to notice that the answers to these questions were requested by 'Jean Dalie (du Lys) Civil Provost of Vaucouleurs in the Diocese of Toul, in the presence of . . . (various dignitaries of Toul) . . . and the vicars and curates of the parishes involved.' The reader will remember that Jehanne la Pucelle, Pierre Darc and Jean Darc were given the surname du Lys after the reappearance of Jehanne in Lorraine, and Jean was appointed Provost of Vaucouleurs. No mention is made of the fact that Jean's name was previously Darc. No member of the Darc family was questioned.

The answers to the questionnaires have a remarkable uniformity, and not one of them mentions that he or she was present at Jehanne's birth. One of them is very interesting because Hauviette, the wife of Gérard de Syna, was the fourteenth witness and gave her age as forty-five. She claimed to be one of Jehanne's special friends and that Jehanne was two or three years older than herself. This would mean that Jehanne was born about 1407. The 'official' birth of Jeanne d'Arc took place in 1412. Another young friend Mengette, the wife of Jean Joyart, said Jehanne was so good and so simple and so pious that she and her friends told her she was too devout. Jean Waterin the fifteenth witness said that often when a number of them were playing together Jehanne frequently went off on her own and it seemed to them that she wanted to talk to God, and he and his pals mocked her and thought it was a good joke.

Jean Colin, who had been vicar at Domremy also testified. He merely said that Jehanne had confessed to him some-times, and he thought she was a good girl, and willingly went to church. He did not mention her visit to him on the way to visit the Duke of Lorraine but said he had seen her mount her horse when leaving Vaucouleurs for Chinon.

Another interesting witness was Bertrand de Poulengy who has my admiration for his respect for the truth. He says Jehanne came from Domremy and had for a father Jacques Darc. He did not know the name of her mother. He was often at their home, and they were good country people. Of questions 4-8 he could only say that he heard that she was a good girl, had a nice figure, often went to church and nearly every Saturday went to Bermont with candles for the chapel. She span, and from time to time helped with the animals and horses. After she had left Domremy he saw her at Vaucouleurs and noticed she went twice a week to confession, she received communion and was very pious. About question 9 he said he had been there for twelve years, before knowing Jehanne – which is the reason why I believe he had been deputed, probably by Yolande, to safeguard her, however unosten-tatiously, long before he undertook to take part in her education.

He mentions that when they began their journey to Chinon Jehanne wanted them all to attend mass the first day, but they persuaded her that it would be too dangerous, as they would only draw attention to themselves, and they were in enemy territory. Each night Jehanne slept with him and Jean de Metz, without taking off any of her clothes. At that time he was young, but he never felt any desire for her, and even if he had, he would not have dared to give way to it, he was so conscious of her goodness. She never swore. He was roused by her words, however, and was convinced that she really had been sent by God. He never saw anything evil in her, she was so good one could honestly say she was a saint.

Jean de Novelonpont de Metz also testified. But he had virtually nothing to say up to the time when she was staying with the Le Royers in Vaucouleurs, prior to her departure to Chinon. He met her in the street and said, 'My dear! What are you doing here? Is the king going to be chased out of his kingdom and are we all to become English?' – (making it clear that they were very well acquainted.) She explained she had been to see Robert de Baudricourt but he wouldn't help. And then she continued, 'No-one else in the world, neither kings nor dukes, nor the daughter of the King of Scotland or anyone else will be able to recover the kingdom of France except me. However, I would much rather spin beside my poor mother, but that is not my job. I've got to go and do it, because that is what my Lord wants me to do.' And I asked her who her Lord was and she said, 'God.' And I promised her then, that with God as my chief, I would lead her to the king. And I asked her when she wanted to go, and she said, 'Today rather than tomorrow. Tomorrow rather than the day after.'

He said they then discussed her clothes, and he undertook to provide her with some that belonged to his sergeant, and the inhabitants of Vaucouleurs provided the rest, including a sword and spurs. And they collected money for a horse which cost sixteen francs to the best of his recollection. She was then given a safe-conduct by Charles Duke of Lorraine, and he went with her as far as Toul, and when she got back to Vaucouleurs he and Bertrand de Poulengy with two of their sergeants and Colet de Vienne, a royal messenger, and an archer called Richard, took the Maid at their own expense – his and Poulengy's – to Chinon. On the way he said he asked her, 'If she really meant what she said and she always answered that they needn't be afraid, she really had a mandate from her brothers in Paradise who told her what she had to do. For four or five years she had been told by her brothers in Paradise and by God that she would have to go to France in order to recover the kingdom. He believed what she said and was inspired by her words and her belief in God. 'I believed she was sent by God. She never swore, and when she wanted to take an oath she just crossed herself.'

Novelonpont confirmed that the three of them had slept together without desire, that they had had to prevent her going off to hear mass, and that when they had arrived at Chinon they had been able to see the King without difficulty, and he had asked them a lot of questions.

As one reads through the contributions to the Trial of Rehabilitation made by many of the people who met and lived with Jehanne during those few months after she arrived at the French court, who had fought with her, or took part in her trial at Rouen, one cannot but feel how cynically she was exploited both in her life and after her death for the benefit of people who owed her so much and gave her so little in return. I believe she seldom regarded her activities as anything but a vehicle for communicating God's will. There was nothing personal about her successes, her métier was simply to convince her companions that provided they believed God was on their side, victory was theirs for the taking. The fact that she herself believed this wholeheartedly, meant that she thrust herself into the front of an assault time and again, behaviour which was amazingly convincing to her troops – obviously she knew what she was talking about, so she could be trusted. The enormous change that occurred in the fortunes of the French forces which followed her being with them, can be largely attributed to just this, and can also account in large measure for the English belief that she was some kind of witch. At the same time it should not be overlooked that she showed a significant understanding of military strategy and tactics. It was a formidable combination, this inalienable belief in victory and a high intelligence.

There were times when she forgot she had missions to perform and indulged her delight in designing and wearing sumptuous clothes, establishing her stable, enjoying her horses and jousting. Meeting her relatives in a social way, as when she stayed with the Alençons, or when the four Jehannes were together in Beaurevoir, fulfilled a need she had felt when young.

One feels sure she herself had no difficulty in endlessly listening to mass – on the contrary, it brought her to some extent into contact with that heavenly world which she was certain was far more important than anything else. I believe she was often uneasy, if not dreading, that if she fell short in any way her Voices might abandon her, and then she would have felt irretrievably lost. She was genuinely shocked when after a victory all her soldiers did not flock into the nearest church to give thanks to God for it. For their own sakes she tried to get everyone shriven before going into battle, and she did her best to discourage camp followers.

The idea that she enjoyed fighting for its own sake may well be wide of the mark. She was continually upset to see young men, French or English, lying wounded, and there are many instances described where she did what she could for all of them. She became furious with people mistreating prisoners or pillaging, and preferred that she and her troops should go hungry rather than eat stolen food. She frequently wept. When Charles had just been crowned and she burst into tears, I think she was just crying from sheer relief.

I doubt if she ever realized that Yolande was deliberately making use of her for her own ends; but she may not have been surprised that she would show zero interest in what happened to her after Charles's anointing. I would expect Yolande, were she asked for her opinion today, to approve of the beatification and sanctification of the myth she and her friends had created, for it was virtually an extension of the same process and with much the same end in view, as her own activities had been. But I think she would have been shocked to hear that the French Government had found it necessary to pay the Vatican whatever the equivalent of 30 million gold francs may have been for the privilege!

How much one would like to know how Jehanne felt about Cauchon, and Cauchon about Jehanne! I wonder if she realized the risks he ran in arranging her escape? And how high a price in fact he paid for doing it? Did she grieve to learn that suddenly and unexpectedly he died in 1442 while he was being shaved, or wonder what had actually happened to him and why? Was it perhaps because he had saved her? Did she understand that in spite of her supposedly being a relapse and heretic, he had allowed her, contrary to all precedent and law, to confess and receive absolution and even communion that fateful morning, almost certainly because he realized it was quite possible if things went wrong that she might be captured while escaping and be killed unshriven?

And what would Jehanne think of Saint Joan of Arc? What a bitter irony that she should be venerated as a virgin! And why not a martyr? Presumably because the Vatican knows the truth. And why should no-one care about the little chapel at Bermont, now neglected and falling into ruin, robbed of its Black Virgin now standing incongruous in the bright crypt of the ostentatious church dedicated to Jeanne d'Arc? It was in Bermont after all where the real Jehanne had prayed so often and with such sincerity, and learned so much from Mère Colette.

Her sound democratic ideas. alas, were three hundred years before their time in France, and many people have argued that if the English had stayed in power there, there need never have been a French Revolution!

When Jehanne married I think she believed that at last, freed of a daunting responsibility which she had faithfully discharged, she could now relax and lead her own life, indulge in her own wishes, and fulfil her own aspirations. The fact that she never experienced the promised miracle in requital, acknowledging how truly she had kept faith, must have been a devastating surprise and disappointment, and one she must always have found hard to understand or accept. Perhaps St Michael managed to convince and comfort her and her husband. I hope he did.

The pathological origin of Jehanne's visions is clearly central to my whole 'Biography'. The fact that she saw a light virtually every time she heard her voices, makes the suggestion that she was pretending to hear voices and see St Catherine and St Margaret extremely unlikely. That really she was referring to people she knew who were giving her advice, (but thought it would be inadvisable to identify them,) seems to me verging on dishonesty by the authors who maintain it. Why do none of them mention that Jehanne repeated over and over again that she almost invariably experienced seeing this light whenever she heard the voice, from the very first time she heard that Voice in the Garden? How can they account for that light otherwise?

That her hallucinations began when they did, was crucial to her whole life afterwards. Admittedly it was unlikely, but unlikely things do occasionally happen.[20] It was a coincidence as unlikely, say, as that of the Spanish woman who won the first prize in a huge national lottery one year, and then drew the winning ticket the following year. The fact is, she did draw it.

Jehanne is rightly regarded as an exceptional person, and her uniqueness resulted from the extreme improbability of that coincidence. She was at an impressionable age when these odd things began to happen to her. She had had a very religious upbringing in a very superstitious age. She had every reason to believe what she heard the Voice in the Garden telling her, and her hallucinations reinforced her belief. Then the exciting and interesting changes that her education took thereafter, confirmed her belief that she had been chosen to carry out God's will.

She learned that she had a status in society that not only made it reasonable for God to have chosen her to carry out His plans, but it must also have improved her morale and added to her self-confidence, enabling her to achieve the almost impossible tasks she had been set.

Her exceptional contact with people like Colette and Yolande whose aims clearly coincided with the advice she was obtaining from her Saints, could only have increased her certainty in the belief that she was destined to spearhead the liberation of France from the invader. Even Saint Louis and Saint Charlemagne she knew were praying for her success!

She was highly intelligent, had a vivid imagination and was possessed of an excellent memory. She was courageous and her courage was enhanced by her hallucinations. I am sure she felt certain when she went into battle that she would not be killed, even though she might be wounded. Whether she was possessed of second sight I cannot say. Who can? Many of her predictions were based, I believe, on remarks made by someone she believed was speaking the truth. For instance one can explain away her belief that she would not escape until she had seen the King of England, as having stemmed from Cauchon mentioning that she was likely to see him when she came to Rouen, combined with the disastrous effect of her second attempt at escaping when she jumped from the tower in Beaurevoir castle. That, her Saints told her, was a sinful thing to have done. To be told that trying to escape was a useless activity anyway until she had seen the English king, was a good way of avoiding feeling one was a coward, or over-estimating in the future the power of one's faith. The firm belief that she would escape from Rouen could well have been based on her belief that God wanted her to complete her missions, as well as Cauchon's early assurances.

One can well understand how she was quite unable to agree that her direct contact with God through her saints was heretical. It had virtually governed her life since she was little more than a child, and had been so successful in carrying out the missions she had undertaken to perform. Her honesty and her courage in maintaining her stance at the trial, and her real inability to understand her accusers' point of view, is what one would expect from her previous conduct and experience. It was how she had behaved in Orleans when Gaucourt tried to keep his gate shut, or when the King's Council tried to avoid threatening Troyes. And God had clearly shown His counsel was reliable then.

Surely the least Jehanne la Pucelle deserves is to be remembered and admired as a real person, imaginative, intelligent, honest and courageous, and that she genuinely tried to establish the Kingdom of Heaven upon Earth.

BIBLIOGRAPHY

Jeanne d'Arc princess royale, Jean Bancal, Robert Laffont, Paris 1971
The Trial of Jeanne d'Arc, W.P. Barrett, John Routledge and Sons, London 1931
Jeanne d'Arc Tertiaire de Saint-Francois, Bessonet-Favre, Bloud et Barral, Paris, 1896
La Verité sur Jeanne d'Arc, Bessonet-Favre, 1897
Jeanne d'Arc était-elle la soeur de Charles VII? Jean Bosler, Edition Scorpion, Paris 1962
Chronique de la Pucelle ou Chronique de Cousinot, edited M. Vallet de Viriville, Paris 1864
Qui était Jeanne d'Arc? G. Crouvezier, Matot-Braine, 1982
Jehanne 1407-1452, Bernard Jean Daulon, Editions Privat – Toulouse 1958
Jeanne d'Arc et la guerre de Trois Cents Ans, Jean Daulon. Editions La Baule, 44501 La Baule
Histoire véridique et merveilleuse de la Pucelle d'Orleans, Maurice David-Darnac. La Table Ronde, 1966
Le Dossier de Jehanne, Maurice David-Darnac, Jean-Jacques Pauvert, 1968
Mais qui es-tu Jehanne d'Arc? Jacques Guérillon, La Pensée Universelle, 1972
Rayonnement de Sainte Colette, Joseph Goulueu, La Colombe-éditions du vieux colombier, Paris 1952
Operation Shepherdess, André Guérin & Jack Palmer White 1960
Jeanne 1407-1449, Charles L. Leclerc, Imprimerie Forézienne, 42110 Feurs
La Vie des Templiers, M. Melville, Paris 1974
Chroniques de Monstrelet, edited by J.A. Buchon, Paris 1827
Jeanne d'Arc à Vaucouleurs Vicomte de Motey, Alencon. 1929
Yolande d'Anjou, la Reine des Quatres Royaumes, Jeanne d'Orliac, Librarie Plon, Paris 1933
Les Procès de Jeanne d'Arc, Raymond Oursel, Editions Denoël, 1959
Jehanne d'Arc n'a pas été brulée, Gérard Pesme, Edition Balzac, 1960
Les Missions secrètes de Jehanne la Pucelle. Pierre de Sermoise, Robert Laffont, Paris 1970
Histoire généalogique de la Maison de France, Ansèlme et Ange
Histoire de France, volumes 1400-1430, C. Villaret, 1763 and 1770

The Holy Blood and the Holy Grail, Michael Baignet, Richard Leigh and Henry Lincoln, Corgi Books 1983
Revolution in Judaea, Hyam Maccoby, Ocean Books 1973
Jesus the Jew, G. Vermes, London 1977

15th century playing cards showing la Pucelle and d'Aulon.

NOTES

NOTE (1) page 16
Porphyria is a hereditary disease caused by an excess of a normally present amino-acid building up in the liver, due to some disturbance of porphyrin metabolism. The victim may suffer from periodic attacks of high blood pressure, a racing pulse, agonising colic, nausea and constipation due to paralysis of the gut, and the peripheral nerves may be affected which supply movement and sensation to all parts of the body, causing painful weakness to the arms and legs. Severe attacks can give rise to giddiness, visual and auditory sensations, mounting excitement and non-stop rambling, irritability and persistent sleeplessness, confusion, typically by night but later also by day, producing delirium, stupor and convulsions. The urine at times is coloured purple, either when it is passed or when it is left to stand, followed later by a clear uncoloured fluid. It is this symptom which has given rise to the name of the disease.

The hereditary factor is a Mendelian dominant, which means that some half of the offspring may expect to inherit the disorder, but it may remain symptomless throughout life, or it may cause attacks of any degree of severity which are always dangerous and may prove fatal. Some victims are sun-sensitive, and the sudden onset that Charles VI exhibited suggests that he may have been one of these. If the patient recovers from an attack he has generally suffered severe weight loss and takes a long time to recover his strength, repeated attacks leading to increasing lethargy and incapacity and mental derangement.

It has been called the Royal Malady, as George III was afflicted with it, and it has been traced back to the Stuarts and Tudors, (See George III and the Mad-Business, by Ida Macalpine and Richard Hunter, Chapter 13, Allen Lane The Penguin Press.) Mary Queen of Scots suffered from it and our James I died of it. Henry VIII in his old age may well have been a victim showing some of the symptoms. Henry VII's grandmother was Catherine, the widow of Henry V. Evidently she was a carrier from her father Charles VI, her son, Henry VI having periodic fits of insanity. After Henry V died, she had a rather scandalous affair with a little known Welshman called Owen Tudor, and their only son Edmund, later legitimised, fathered our Henry VII.

NOTE (2) page 22
Jean Jacoby suggests that this may have been one of the reasons for the

singular rule that French queens had to have their confinements in public, a custom that persisted up to the time of Marie-Antoinette.

NOTE (3a) page 27

The arms of the Darc family were 'D'azure à un arc posé en fasce, chargé en trois flèches entrecroissées les pointes ferrues et plumetées d'argent, la troisième d'argent ferrée et plumetée d'or, au chef d'argent chargé d'un lion passant de gueules.' In ordinary language this can be described as a shield the lower two thirds being blue, carrying a bow bearing three crossed arrows pointing upwards, two are tipped and feathered in silver, one is tipped in silver and feathered in gold. The top third of the shield is silver bearing a red lion with the right foreleg raised.

NOTE (3b) page 27

The suggestion that Isabelle or her mother had made a pilgrimage to Rome is unlikely as the pope had lived in Avignon for some seventy years. Some say that a pilgrimage to Puy was sufficient to become entitled to adopt the name Romée.

NOTE (4) page 30

The Bourlemont castle was let in 1420 to Jacques Darc and Jehan Bizet from June 24th 1419 for nine years. Signed April 2nd, 1420, Archives of Meurthe-et-Moselle, Reference Layette – Ruppe II No 28, Journal de la Société d'Archéologie Lorraine de janvier et février 1889. I think it likely Yolande suggested this move.

NOTE (5) page 50

The Voice in the Garden has been ascribed before to Colette, but that she was deliberately attempting to mislead Jehanne into believing that she was hearing a Voice from Heaven has not to my knowledge been suggested before. I suspect it was Yolande's idea, and this is almost confirmed by the papal secretary Silvius Piccolimini, later Pius II, quoted on p.177. I think the order that the event had to be kept secret from everyone, including parents and confessor, suggests a human rather than a divine prohibition too. One can imagine Yolande, being told about what had happened, asking why this ban had been included, 'What would I have answered if she had asked me if I believed it really was a voice from Heaven?' Although Jehanne only said in Rouen that she was told she must go to church often, I think she was actually told to go to the Hermitage of Sainte-Marie in Bermont, where Colette habitually stayed when she was in the neighbourhood. Several people testified that they often saw Jehanne running off there.

NOTE (6) page 51

I hope no-one will suggest that because Jehanne experienced hallucinations she was therefore mad. She was absolutely sane, but because of her religious upbringing and beliefs, combined with her lack of medical knowledge, she was readily mistaken as she was meant to be, in her interpretation.

I owe this theory of a tuberculoma causing Jehanne's hallucinations to the paper published by Professor Butterfield and his wife Isobel (now Lord and Lady Butterfield) in History Today, 1958 page 628. Contrary to the statement made in Guérillon's book that they claimed she had a tubercular abcess in her brain, they make it quite clear that it was a tuberculoma, which is virtually a neutral body, in her temple. So many of Jehanne's experiences can be explained by it, and they are so difficult to explain otherwise – unless one assumes they really did emanate from Heaven. (The pope denied this and it was because Jehanne insisted that they did, that she was condemned as a heretic.) It is typical too, that such hallucinations become more frequent as time passes. She claimed to have three or more visions in a day during the trial, whereas initially she had about three a week.

I do not agree with the Butterfields that Jehanne showed other tubercular symptoms. She seems on the contrary to have been very strong and healthy. The only time she is mentioned as being ill, was when she ate the stuffed carp Cauchon sent her, (I am sure with the best of intentions!) The doctor was told he simply must not allow her to die. She recovered in spite of being bled. When she was wounded her wounds healed up quickly, and she showed amazing stamina and had been known to keep on her armour for days at a stretch, even though it weighed fifty pounds or more. I also do not think her lack of menstruation was tubercular in origin, (see NOTE 8).

NOTE (7) page 52

Karen Horney in her *Neurotic Personality of our Time* page 96 (Kegan Paul, Trench, Trubner and Co. Ltd., 1937) in a discussion of anxiety and its reassurance, says, 'The more unbearable the anxiety, the more thorough the protective means have to be . . . Securing affection in any form may serve as a powerful protection against anxiety and . . . submissiveness to the demands of some powerful person also gives reassurance. To comply with these demands will be the determining motive for all behaviour. This attitude may take the form of being "Good" although the connotation of "good" varies with the demands.' Jehanne promised to remain a virgin until she had fulfilled her missions to God's satisfaction.

NOTE (8) page 55

Her lack of menstruation was due, it would seem, to her suffering from a syndrome known as testicular feminisation. It arises when a male foetus with one X and one Y chromosome is insensitive to the male hormone testosterone. The individual grows up looking like a woman with delicate skin, light voice, well-formed breasts and small waist, but no womb develops and the vagina varies in different individuals from apparently normal to nearly closed. Pubic hair is absent.

The medical doctor Delachambre who attended Jehanne when she was suffering from food poisoning examined her – and people were normally stark naked when they were in bed in those days – and described her as 'narrow' with the vaginal lips almost joined and '*jeune fille*', meaning pubic hair had not developed in spite of her age. Her chaplain, Jean Pasquerel, testifying at the Trial of Rehabilitation said, 'I know that on her arrival, before she saw the king, she was examined twice by ladies in order to find out if she was a man or a woman and a complete virgin or not. They discovered she was a woman and a complete virgin, and in spite of her age had no pubic hair'.

That Jehanne was one of these individuals was pointed out by an American doctor, Robert Greenblatt, in Diagnosis, March 1983, page 7. I do not think there is any reason to suppose that this was why she dressed in men's clothes, as 'cross-dressing' is not associated with this condition. I agree with Jehanne when she claimed it was more appropriate when she was on active service or in prison. Naturally 'God so ordained it' when she found herself in such a situation. It should perhaps be noted that *une pucelle* meant *une fille,* a girl. No state of virginity was implied in the word. Spelt with a capital P it was the equivalent, in a way, of the title Bastard, used almost as a surname.

NOTE (9) page 64

Hyam Maccoby points out that to a Jew the title Messiah (Greek = Christos) is not a divine title. It simply means anointed. It was given to two Jewish officials, the King and the High Priest, who were anointed with oil at their inauguration ceremonies. Every Jewish king of the House of David was known as Messiah or Christ. Nowadays the word 'Christ' has become so imbued with the idea of deity that it is hard for a non-Jew to appreciate what these words meant to a Jew when Jesus was alive. In those days the idea of a *divine* Messiah was unknown. Similarly 'Son of God' was simply a royal title and likewise carried no connotation of divinity. 'This is my beloved Son' is taken from the Coronation Psalm, (Ps ii). The idea of a human being who was also divine was unthinkable and blasphemous, (see *Revolution in Judea* by Hyam Maccoby, Ocean Books 1973, Chapter 9 pp346-355. For an interesting discussion of the anointing of Jesus as King, see ibid Chapter 12.)

NOTE (10) page 65

When the Romans were ruling Europe many of their temples were dedicated to a mother goddess carved in dark hardwood, somewhat less than life-size, often crowned and holding a sceptre in her right hand. Her left arm encircled a baby holding a white bird. When an Irish monk, Saint Columbanus, came to France proselytizing, he readily grafted his new ideas on to theirs, as it was easy to see the Virgin with Jesus holding the Holy Ghost in the existing statue. These especially venerated ancient carvings became known as Black Virgins.

NOTE (11) page 67

René d'Anjou was Grandmaster of the *Priory of Sion (Nautonnier du Prieuré du Sion)* from 1418-1480. *The Holy Blood & The Holy Grail*, Corgi Books 1983 p133 of Chapter 9.

NOTE (12) page 79

It has been suggested that Jehanne showed Charles a gold ring bearing the Orleans arms that Louis was supposed to have been wearing when he was assassinated, and which Isabeau is supposed to have sent to Jehanne as evidence of her parentage. There is no mention in Chartier's account as far as I am aware, of Jehanne showing him a ring on this occasion, though she did have such a ring at some time.

NOTE (13) page 80
Although the Commissioners at Poitiers were informed that Jehanne and Charles were full brother and sister, and who their parents were, they were doubtless sworn to secrecy. Some close relatives and their confidants also knew, but for the most part this was kept secret. Jehanne also revealed to the Commissioners some of her 'revelations', 'if it was God's will to do so.'

But during the trial in Rouen she refused to answer the same queries unless she received renewed permission, advising her questioners instead to get a copy of the *Livre de Poitiers* if they wanted replies she had sworn not to reveal. For centuries it was supposed that the *Livre* was lost or had been destroyed. But we know now that it did divulge her real parentage. How this knowledge came about is a very revealing story, well told in the Appendices of Gérard Presme's book *Jehanne d'Arc n'a pas été brulée* and in David-Darnac's *Le Dossier de Jehanne*. In brief, a noted Catholic historian and writer called Edouard Schneider, a devout priest, who died in August 1960, had found the *Livre de Poitiers* in the Vatican library, some time between 1933 and 1935. It was not in fact a book but a report written on separate sheets at the time of the interrogation of Jehanne, a record of the questions asked her and her replies. The commissioners were unwilling to admit that her visions were from God, so they were unable to recommend that the king should rely on her. However, he insisted on two Franciscan monks being sent to Domremy and Vaucouleurs. They returned with a report that stated that every inhabitant of Domremy had attested that she was the daughter of Isabeau of Bavaria and the late Duke of Orleans. This report was added to the other papers.

Schneider made a copy of the book including the 'capital piece' – the report from Domremy. He kept this with his belongings in his lodgings in Rome. But when the librarian Monseigneur Tisserant discovered what he had found, he made him swear that he would not publish it, 'because it would destroy the legend'!

Schneider had been a close friend of Marshall Pétain, and as such was suspected of being a collaborator, so he took refuge in the Vatican. But he decided to return to Paris when an amnesty was declared. For safekeeping he left all his possessions packed in four boxes with an old friend, the Marchioness de Félici who lived in the Zenardeli Palace. All his documents were in one of the boxes. When he wrote to her asking for them to be sent on to him, he received a letter saying that she had just died, and there were only three boxes there. He rushed back to Rome, and his precious documents were not to be found. The conclusion has been drawn that in her last confession the old lady had revealed the existence of these documents, and as a result they had been stolen.

Schneider wrote a book entitled *Jehanne d'Arc et ses Lys,* published in 1952.

It was put on the Black List, and very few copies were sold. I have never been able to see one although the University Library did its best to borrow one for me. Mme Collignon's copy has been stolen. The book consists of two parts, the first the orthodox story, the second the historical Jehanne la Pucelle, based upon the arguments put forward by Jean Jacoby (1932), and Jean Grimod (1952), but no reference is made to the author's Vatican discovery. One gathers from endless conversations he had with friends, that he felt obliged not to mention it because he had no evidence in support, his precious copy having disappeared. One has to end this sad story by relating that to the end of his life poor *'Edouard Schneider n'avait aucun autre sujet de conversation et ne parlait que de sa découverte du matin au soir,'* (He had no other subject of conversation and only talked about his discovery from morning to night.)

No one else has since been allowed to see this interesting historical document which one hopes has been safely hidden again and not destroyed.

Of the secret concerning Charles's marriage to Marie d'Anjou I do not believe Jehanne's interrogators had the least suspicion. But when Charles spoke of 'Their Secret' in the garden of the House of the Annunciation, possibly the last time they met, I am sure this was what he alluded to. Certainly it was not to a wonderful golden crown with a delicious odour!

NOTE (14) page 96

In some places where there is a considerable area of water, the relative temperatures of the air and the water determine whether or not there is any wind and if there is, its direction. When the temperature of the air becomes the greater the wind will suddenly blow in one direction, and the reverse is true when the water becomes warmer.

NOTE (15) page 143

Jean Quicherat made a painstaking collection of the official Latin trial records which he began publishing in 1841, occupying many volumes. Raymond Oursel published *Les Procès de Jeanne d'Arc (édition denoël)* in 1959, a modern French translation of both the trial in Rouen and the Rehabilitation trial after Jehanne's death. His translation of the Trial at Rouen occupies some 105 pages. He gives the questions and answers that comprised the interrogations including the preliminary sessions, in direct speech instead of the original indirect form. A summary of the indictment and the Act of Accusation is also given, and a brief summary of the subsequent legal proceedings and the execution. A much more satisfactory account by W.P. Barrett *The Trial of Jeanne D'Arc*, (John Routledge and Sons, London,) was published in 1931. This is closer to the indirect form of the original documents, and the whole book of some 350 pages, which includes all the original letters of the assessors, leaves a very different impression of the trial, as it shows why her judges were unable to accept that she was inspired by God. Briefly they believed that God would have performed at least one miracle had He been involved, and since that was not to be found, they were driven to the conclusion that her visions were either the result of her human imagination or due to an evil spirit.

NOTE (16) page 174

Between 1430 and 1432 the archives of Rouen give the names of five witches who were burned in the Old Market Place there. Their names are to be found in the *Livres des Comptes des Domaines* together with the cost of the wood burned and the salaries of the executioners. The witches were called Jeanne de la Turquenne, Jeanne Vannerie, Jeanne de la Guillorée, Alice de la Rousse and Caroline-la-Ferte. No mention is made of Jehanne la Pucelle, Jehanne Romée, or Jehanne Darc. No execution took place on May 30th 1432 according to these records.

NOTE (17) page 176

'Orthodox' books either ignore Jehanne's history after the trial at Rouen or attribute it to a successful impersonator, a 'false Joan of Arc'. John Holland Smith, an English author, even invents one who called herself Claude des Armoises! And a French one, Bessonet-Favre, produces a twin sister, also called Claude if I remember correctly, who took over when Jehanne had been burned.

It has been justly pointed out that it shows a singular arrogance on the part of people who are living five hundred years after her death, and who never ever set eyes on Jehanne, to be so sure that the inhabitants of Orleans who worshipped her, her brother Charles VII, Yolande, her foster mother and two foster brothers, the Metzian gentleman who thanks to Jehanne was granted the singular honour of being knighted immediately after the king had been crowned, her comrades in arms and the countless people who knew her while she was living with the French Court, were all successfully bamboozled over a period of sixteen years. It is also worth remembering that aristocrats did not choose wives without pedigree in those days, though illegitimacy in itself did not carry the stigma that it later acquired. No-one, as far as I know, has yet identified the high-born lady who managed to convince Robert des Armoises that she was the Pucelle de France, or who misled the Duchess of Luxembourg that she was her niece.

NOTE (18) page 181

The marriage certificate was discovered in 1645 in the archives of the branch of the Armoises living in the castle of Jaulny by Father Vignier de l'Oratoire, according to an entry in the Mercure Galant in 1683 and then again in Mercure de France in 1723. A contract of marriage signed by Jehanne la Pucelle and Robert des Armoises was found by a notary in Fresnes-en-Woèvres who was researching for Anatole France in 1907. This was unfortunately lost when the village was totally destroyed in the Great War. The Armoises house in Metz was demolished in 1854 when the square was enlarged. The house was decorated by a double coat of arms – that of la Pucelle and of Robert des Armoises.

NOTE (19) page 181

Built on an escarpment which dominates the valley where the Rupt de Mad runs, the castle of Jaulny belonged to the family des Armoises from

214

1357, a date at which Collart proceeded to effect an exchange of land with his son-in-law. 'In this year 1357, Collart des Armoises, knight, Marie de Chambley his wife, MADE AN EXCHANGE of all that which the said Collart had at la Bouche, against that of the said Jamais had at Jaulny and at Grange au Bois' . . . (Dom Calmet: geneaology of the Armoises, page CLIX) . . . The property stayed during more than a century in the hands of the same family. In 1457 there was a treaty between Simon and Ferri des Armoises, equerries father and son, lords of Jaulny, by which they settled their differences with Simonin, Ferri and Jacques des Armoises Lords of Fléville en Barrois at Jaulny . . . The castle came up for sale in the late nineteenth century. The new owner was told by the villagers that there was a portrait of La Pucelle in the castle but it had been hidden to prevent its destruction. He searched for this but did not find it. The subsequent owner asked an architect to undertake some repairs and he noticed a crack in the plaster over the fireplace in the salon. This fell away when he was examining it and revealed a handsome chimney piece with two profile portraits facing each other of Jehanne and her husband.

NOTE (20) page 204
I suppose it is not impossible that had Jehanne acquired a tuberculoma in a suitable position the shock of realising that she had been singled out by an angel or a demon could have precipitated a hallucination simply as a result of increased adrenalyn and high blood pressure.

GLOSSARY

Charles VI 1368-1380-1422
>   The king of France when Joan was born. Subject to periodic
>   fits of madness. Married to Isabeau of Bavaria 1385.

Isabeau of Bavaria 1371-1435
>   Had twelve children, ten by her husband Charles VI, two by
>   her brother-in-law Louis, Duke of Orleans, viz. Charles VII
>   and Jehanne la Pucelle.

Louis Duke of Orleans 1372-1407
>   Brother of Charles VI. Married to Valentine Visconti,
>   Duchess of Milan. They had two sons, Charles and Jean. By
>   his mistress Mariette d'Englen he had a son 'the Bastard'
>   later called Dunois, who was adopted by his wife, and two
>   children by Isabeau: Charles (later Charles VII) and
>   Jehanne la Pucelle. Louis was assassinated by Jean sans
>   Peur.

Louis Duke of Guyenne 1397-1415
>   The dauphin. Married Marguerite of Burgundy. Murdered
>   by the Burgundians. Stepbrother of Jehanne.

Jean Duke of Touraine 1398-1417
>   Married to Jacqueline of Bavaria. Dauphin after his
>   brother's death. The Armagnacs murdered him. Step-
>   brother of Jehanne.

Charles VII 1403-1422-1461
>   Originally Count of Ponthieu. Legally he was the son of
>   Charles VI but his real parents were Queen Isabeau and

Louis Duke of Orleans. Became dauphin when his brother Jean was murdered. Married Marie, elder daughter of Yolande Duchess of Anjou. Brother of Jehanne. Crowned in Poitiers 1422, in Rheims 1429.

Charles Duke of Orleans 1391-1465
Son of Louis Duke of Orleans. Captured at Agincourt and held for ransom in London for twenty-five years. Famous for his lyrical poetry. Stepbrother of Jehanne.

Duke of Alençon
A cousin of Charles VII, married to daughter of the exiled Charles Duke of Orleans. Jehanne was his aunt by marriage.

Dunois
Illegitimate son of Louis. His mother died in childbirth, and Louis's wife willingly adopted him and brought him up as her own son. He became a distinguished soldier. Known as The Bastard of Orleans until he was ennobled as Count Dunois in 1422 – it was almost like a surname, and Jehanne's Maid or La Pucelle was much the same. Stepbrother of Jehanne.

Michelle of France 1395-1422
Daughter of Charles VI, married to Philippe le Bon, son of Jean sans Peur. Stepsister of Jehanne.

Catherine of France 1401-1438
Youngest daughter of Charles VI, married to King Henry V 1420, mother of King Henry VI. Stepsister of Jehanne.

Jehanne de Luxembourg
An aunt of Jehanne, godmother of Charles VII. Was living in Ligny's castle Beaurevoir when Jehanne was imprisoned there. Died in her castle at Crotoy, after having Jehanne fetched to see her there. Made Jean de Ligny her heir when he promised not to sell her to the English.

Elizabeth of Luxembourg
Widow of an uncle of Philippe le Bon, Duke of Burgundy, who gave Jehanne and her 'brothers' hospitality for five months in Arlon. Jehanne married Robert des Armoises while living with her.

217

Jean sans Peur, Duke of Burgundy 1371-1419
>Had one son Philippe le Bon and three daughters. He was a cousin of Louis Duke of Orleans whom he assassinated in 1407. Unscrupulously signed a treaty with King Henry V acknowledging him to be the rightful heir to the French throne. Jean was assassinated at Montereau by Tanguy du Chatel in revenge for Louis's murder. All Jean's children shared the same great-grandfather with Jehanne – Jean le Bon who died in 1364.

Philippe le Bon, Duke of Burgundy 1396-1467
>Son of Jean sans Peur. Married Michelle, daughter of Charles VI. Became an ally of the English after his father's murder until he signed the Treaty of Arras in 1435. Cousin of Jehanne.

Anne Duchess of Bedford
>Youngest daughter of Jean sans Peur. Married the Duke of Bedford Regent of France in 1424. They lived in Bouvreuil castle in Rouen. She died in 1432. She was a Third Order *Dame très Discrète*. Cousin of Jehanne.

Duke of Bedford
>Brother of Henry V. After Henry V died the Regency of France was offered to Philippe Duke of Burgundy. He refused it. Bedford then became Regent. He married Philippe's youngest sister, Anne. His headquarters in France were in the castle Bouvreuil in Rouen. The Duke of Warwick was responsible for its defence.

Yolande Duchess of Anjou 1379-1442
>Daughter of the King of Aragon. Inherited her mother's Duchy of Bar. In 1400 married Louis II Duke of Anjou, King of Naples and King of Jerusalem. He died in 1417. They had five children, Louis, Marie, René, Yolande and Charles. The duchess was the head of the Franciscan Third Order in France. I believe she made herself responsible for looking after Jehanne from the time she was born. Yolande and Jehanne were both great-grandchildren of King Jean-le-Bon of France.

René d'Anjou, Duke of Bar and Lorraine 1418-1480
>Second son of Yolande and Louis d'Anjou. Married Isabelle of Lorraine. René was King of Jerusalem and Grand Master

of the Priory of Sion. Cousin of Jehanne.

Robert des Armoises 1405-1450
Cousin of Robert de Baudricourt's wife. When he was twenty he went to the Baudricourt's wedding in Vaucouleurs and may have met Jehanne there. He was widowed when he met Jehanne in 1436 at her aunt's house in Arlon, Luxembourg. They were married there a few months later. They had no children, though he had had children by his first wife.

UNRELATED PEOPLE OF IMPORTANCE TO JEHANNE IN DOMREMY

Colette de Corbie 1380-1446
At first a recluse, later reformed the Franciscan sisterhood of the Poor Clares. Her headquarters were in Besançon. Had great influence in the Third Order of the Franciscans. Probably she chose the Darc family to foster Jehanne in response to Yolande's request. Largely responsible for Jehanne's upbringing in Domremy. Colette was later sanctified.

Darc (Jehanne)
The sister-in-law of Jacques Darc who made contact with Isabeau in June 1407 and was present at Jehanne's birth as a lady-in-waiting. She was one of the party taking the baby to Domremy, and was a godmother at her christening there.

Darc (Jacques)
The Darc family had borne arms for at least two centuries when poverty due to the Hundred Years War and the Black Death had made him derogate and become a breeder of cattle. Later his noble status was restored. Married Isabelle de Vouton, normally called Isabelle Romée. They had three children Pierre, Catherine and Petit Jehan, the last born after Jehanne was brought to them.

Isabelle Romée
Wife of Jacques. She came of a deeply religious family and was a keen member of the Third Order and friend of Colette de Corbie. When she was widowed she was invited to live in

219

Orleans and there the town granted her a pension paid to 'the mother of Jehanne la Pucelle' until 1449, after which it was paid to 'the mother of the late Jehanne la Pucelle.'

Darc (Pierre)

The elder child of the Darc family when Jehanne was fostered. He accompanied her to Chinon, and stayed with her throughout her active military life. He was captured at Compiegne with her, and accompanied her when she returned to France to fight again after her marriage. He, his brother and Jehanne were ordered to adopt du Lys as their surname after Jehanne reappeared in Lorraine, and they were all permitted to use the coat of arms originally granted exclusively to Jehanne la Pucelle after she had liberated Orleans. Pierre was made a member of the prestigious Order of the Porcupine. He was rewarded for his loyalty to Jehanne by the king and the Duke of Orleans.

Darc (Petit Jehan)

The younger son of the Darcs, born soon after Jehanne's arrival in the family. He was in the king's employ for some years, and was later appointed Civil Provost of Vaucouleurs.

Poulengy (Bertrand de)

Probably concerned with Jehanne's security when she was growing up in Domremy. When she was destined to become a leader he taught her to handle horses and weapons. He was a member of the garrison in Vaucouleurs and part of her escort to Chinon. He became one of her equerries.

Novelonpont (Jean de, also known as Jean de Metz)

Jehanne's tutor in military strategy and tactics. He was put in charge of the escort who accompanied her when she went to Chinon, and later became one of her equerries.

Baudricourt (Robert de)

He was in charge of the castle at Vaucouleurs, responsible for the security of the Royal Domain and the villages in Bar. Towards the end of her time in the Bar he found her lodgings in Vaucouleurs with some simple people called Catherine and Henri le Royer. He was instrumental in arranging Jehanne's visit to Lorraine, and organized her

escort for her subsequent journey to the French Court. He
joined her personal force in the liberation of Orleans.

PEOPLE IMPORTANT IN JEHANNE'S LIFE
AFTER DOMRÉMY

Aulon (Jean d')
> Distinguished military expert assigned to Jehanne as her
> major-domo when she took up residence in the Coudray
> Tower in Chinon. One time personal bodyguard to Charles
> VI. He accompanied her thereafter in her campaigns and
> she doubtless benefited from his military experience. He
> was captured when she was and he and Pierre Darc were
> allowed to attend her in Beaurevoir – a sign that her rank
> was acknowledged.

Bréhal (Jean) Head of the French Inquisition after Jehanne's death in
1449.

Cauchon (Pierre)
> Bishop of Beauvais, chaplain to the Duke of Bedford,
> Archdeacon of Rheims Cathedral, one time secretary to
> Isabeau and Rector of the University of Paris. He managed
> to be on good terms with most factions in France. He was a
> brilliant negotiator. To protect Jehanne from death at the
> hands of Dominicans in Paris he arranged for her trial to
> take place in Rouen with himself as judge. He also
> organized her escape from death on the stake. In 1439 he
> mediated the cessation of hostilities between England and
> France.

Clovis
> The most famous Merovingian ruler, and the earliest
> French king to become a Roman Catholic. He was baptized
> in Rheims with oil sent from Heaven. From the time of the
> coronation of Saint Louis IX in Rheims, all the French kings
> except one were crowned there and anointed with this oil.
> This was important as it proved that they were chosen by
> God to rule France.

Delachambre
> The medical doctor who attended Jehanne when she was
> suffering from food poisoning. He noticed that she

221

exhibited no pubic hair and the entrance to her vagina was very small.

Du Guesclin 1320-1380

One of France's great soldiers. While head of Charles V's army he almost managed to drive the English out of France. He became the clandestine head of the Templars after they had been disbanded and where possible had become Franciscans. He bequeathed his sword to Jehanne's father. By sending a gold ring to Du Guesclin's widow Jehanne was indicating her political intentions.

Erard (Guillaume)

One of the assessors apparently critical of Cauchon, who took an active part in Jehanne's trial, and read the sermon before she was persuaded to abjure.

Flavy (Guillaume de)

The governor of Compiegne, a half-brother of Regnault de Chartres and a friend of La Tremouille, active in the plans to bring about the capture of Jehanne by the Burgundians.

Gaucourt (Jean de)

Secretary and financier to Charles Duke of Orleans, allowed to visit him in London whenever he pleased. He approved of Yolande.

Gaucourt (Raoul de)

Governor of Orleans when Jehanne liberated it in spite of his efforts to prevent her. A friend of La Tremouille.

Gerson (Cardinal Jehan)

Renowned theologian, one-time Rector of the University of Paris, enthusiastic supporter of the Duchess of Anjou, probably responsible for the monks' vital Domremy Report in the *Livre de Poitiers* affirming Jehanne's royal parentage.

Giac (Pierre de)

A friend of La Tremouille. They were sent with another young man to see that Isabeau did not escape when she was exiled in a convent near Tours because of her outrageous promiscuity. Later they helped her to escape and took her to Jean sans Peur's fortified castle in Troyes. Giac was involved in the assassination of Jean sans Peur so he then left the Burgundian court. Later he became Charles VII's favourite. He then murdered his wife and married his mistress. Tremouille arranged his assassination with Richemont's approval. La Tremouille married Giac's widow two months later.

Graverand (Jean)
> The French Inquisitor, who should have taken a leading role in Jehanne's trial. He took himself off to Coutance at the beginning of it in order to avoid all papal responsibility for whatever might occur. It was very important for Cauchon because had Graverand been present it would have been necessary for him to have insisted that Jehanne should be moved to an ecclesiastical prison instead of staying in her safe quarters in Bouvreuil.

Ladvenu (Martin)
> A Dominican monk who seems to have been close to Cauchon, and to have seen Jehanne on various occasions when she had cause for complaint. He and another Dominican, Toutmouillé, accompanied Massieu when he delivered the death sentence to Jehanne on May 14th 1431 in her dungeon. Ladvenu consented to hear her confess and gave her absolution (both were illegal), but he refused her communion until Cauchon, (to his surprise) gave him permission for this as well. Massieu and Ladvenu left Jehanne after this, but Toutmouillé stayed until Cauchon arrived and asked him to leave him alone with Jehanne.

La Tremouille (Georges de)
> Charles's favourite for many years. Jehanne's and Yolande's most formidable enemy at the French Court. He abominated and feared Jehanne's democratic ideas, and was completely unscrupulous. He was really a Burgundian agent at the Court.

La Tremouille (Jean de)
> Georges' brother, chamberlain to the Duke of Burgundy.

Le Maçon (Robert)
> Chancellor to the Dauphin Charles. He supported Yolande.

Le Maître (Jean)

The local representative of the Inquisition. He was no keener to attend the court sessions than Graverand had been. The court opened on January 9th, he turned up for the first time on March 13th! It seems he was never consulted, and was not present when the last session occurred. Nor was he present at the execution.

Ligny (Jean de)

A vassal of Burgundy. Jehanne was captured by one of Ligny's archers, and was therefore handed over to him. Jehanne Duchess of Luxembourg made Ligny her heir only after he promised not to accept money from the English in exchange for Jehanne la Pucelle. To his wife's disgust, shortly after he became the immensely rich Duke of Luxembourg, he accepted 10,000 francs on behalf of the Duke of Burgundy for her, ostentatiously paying the money into the Duke of Burgundy's coffer. However, he probably knew this was the only way to safeguard her from the Dominicans who intended to burn her for heresy. He later came with a delegation to Rouen to offer to ransom her if she would promise not to take up arms again. She refused.

Louve (Nicholas)

A prominent citizen of Metz, and important member of the Third Order. Thanks to Jehanne he had enjoyed the singular honour of being knighted immediately after Charles VII had been crowned. Five years after her 'execution' Jehanne reappeared in Lorraine and sought out this gentleman who immediately recognized her and vouched for her identity. He provided her with a horse and introduced her to his friends, and gave her useful help and publicity.

Machet (Gérard)

Charles VII's confessor. A revered theologian, one-time rector of the University of Paris. A strong supporter of the Duchess of Anjou. He greatly disapproved of the ostentatious wealth of cardinals and bishops.

Manchon (Guillaume) and Courcelles (Thomas de)

The two recorders of what took place in the court trying Jehanne.

Massieu (Jean)
> The Usher – responsible for taking Jehanne to court and returning her to Bouvreuil.

Monstrelet (Enguerrand de)
> Official historian to the Duke of Burgundy. Famous for failing to remember a word of what was said when Burgundy interviewed Jehanne after she was captured at Compiegne.

Rais (Gilles de)
> An immensely rich man who supported Jehanne's attack on Orleans, and later staged an incredibly extravagant pageant to celebrate it. After she was married and returned to France to pacify the countryside with him, they then attacked the English with considerable success in the Bayonne and round Bordeaux. He died much later in disgrace, probably a victim of the Inquisition.

Regnault de Chartres Archbishop of Rheims
> Friend and collaborator of Georges La Tremouille.

Richard (Brother)
> A demagogic preacher with French rather than Burgundian sympathies.

Richemont (Arthur) Constable of France
> Brother of the Duke of Brittany. Yolande had complete confidence in him, but Charles hated him and encouraged by La Tremouille undermined his authority entirely for some seven years. He married the first dauphin's widow Marguerite of Burgundy.

Tanguy du Chatel
> An enthusiastic Orleanist, who saved Charles VII when he was a little boy from the Cabochian rioters. Later he organized the disastrous assassination of Jean sans Peur. His presence at Charles's court proving impossible as a result, Yolande arranged for him to receive some salt taxes in Provence as long as he stayed there.

Xaintrailles
> One of the most enthusiastic military supporters of Jehanne. He was the only one to turn up when she had

asked for volunteers to accompany her to help the people of Compiegne. He was captured at the same time as Jehanne, but soon ransomed.

LIST OF ILLUSTRATIONS

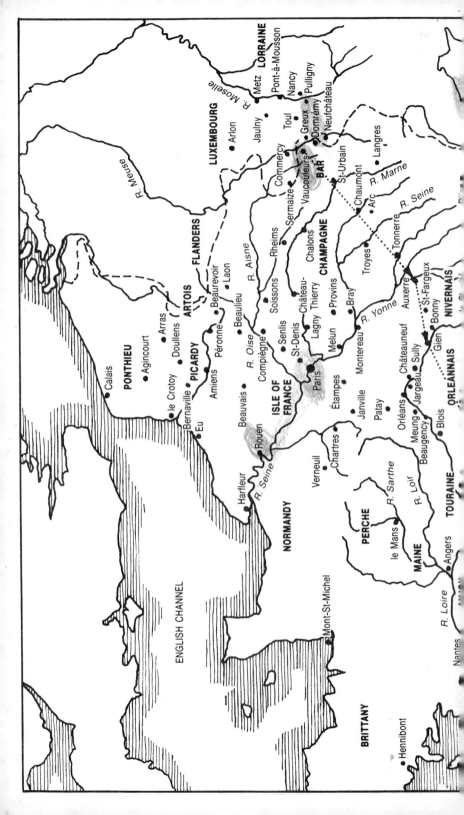